4: The Four Principles of a Debt Free Life

By
John R. Schneider, III
& David Auten

Copyright © 2014 by John R. Schneider, III & David Auten

ISBN 978-0-7414-9964-6

Printed in the United States of America

Published October 2014

INFINITY PUBLISHING
1094 New DeHaven Street, Suite 100
West Conshohocken, PA 19428-2713
Toll-free (877) BUY BOOK
Local Phone (610) 941-9999
Fax (610) 941-9959
Info@buybooksontheweb.com
www.buybooksontheweb.com

Table of Contents

Introduction

As you will see in the first two sections, the principles that are the foundation of this book came to us through our own, personal journey with debt. We found ourselves in the same situation many Americans face today. Something was seriously wrong with our spending habits, and we had the realization that we could become debt free if we made some minor and some major changes to those habits.

Our purpose with this book is the help you become Money Conscious. By the time you finish reading this book, you'll have the tools to help you eliminate your own debt, sustain a debt free lifestyle, and achieve financial success by virtue of four universal principles. We're certain that these four principles will reduce your debt to $0.

What are you waiting for? With a little time, focus and understanding, you too can be debt free and on your way to financial success. Our stories should help you see your opportunities.

We are where we are today because of the decisions we made yesterday. Likewise, we will be where we are tomorrow because of the decisions we make today. Here are the keys to financial freedom.

Dedication

We dedicate this book to each individual who accepts personal responsibility for his or her financial situation and chooses to not let his or her mistakes be someone else's burden.

Acknowledgements

We would first like to acknowledge the support and motivation provided to us by our editor, Nancy Hutchins. Her affirmations helped us finish what may have otherwise been another incomplete book on a hard-drive.

We also want to thank our friends, family and colleagues who provided emotional support when we decided to take a chance in getting this book to the public. Special thanks go to our friends who helped make this happen. Thanks to Edward Young who used his summer vacation to provide us with final edits. Thanks to Edith Wentz whose artistic ability created a great book cover. Finally, thanks to Kevin Zolitor who let us take advantage of his hobby and took our photo for the back cover.

More personally, we would like to thank and acknowledge each other's efforts in writing this book. This has been a labor of love. Each of us, at various stages, needed to motivate the other. Neither of us could have achieved this alone.

Prologue

If you've picked up or downloaded this book, you're wondering if you can improve your financial situation. For many, this is daunting. For many, understanding money and finance seems too difficult and is the reason why you're in your current financial situation. Believe us, even the savviest financial guru can be a financial nightmare when it comes to managing their money.

Despite having had thirteen years of experience working in financial services between the two of us, we were financial messes. We were two thirty-something professionals with $51,000 of combined debt, living in a basement apartment. After reaching our rock-bottom, we had a heart-to-heart and made the decision to not continue on the road we had been for so long. Concurrently, we had the inferior feeling of not keeping up with our peers. How were they able to live the life we wanted to live, yet weren't finding themselves in the same financial situation? Why were we living in a basement apartment when they were each buying houses larger than the other.

This book is about our journey of getting out of debt. While on that journey, we discovered four principles necessary for anyone to rid themselves of debt and stay debt free. We wrote this book to help people just like us. Whether you have a small amount of debt or more debt than you can wrap your head around, these principles apply to you. Our hope is that this book will save you time, frustration, and most importantly, money.

Most of this book was put together over seven years using our personal experiences. We incorporated our combined financial services experience, which now totals 30 years. Much has changed economically and politically in the U.S and globally since we acquired and got out of debt, and wrote this book. Regardless, these four principles hold true.

We hope this book meets our goal of helping you get out of and stay out of debt. We hope that students, whether in high school or college, read this book and apply these principles to their lives. If either of these happen, our investment in writing this will be worthwhile.

Our suggestion for getting the most out of this book is to first read it from start to finish. After reading it in its entirety, start from the beginning again and complete the steps that we've outlined. Go through the book more methodically in subsequent readings, apply what you learn and see your financial situation improve.

Chapter One:

Personal Stories
About the Authors

David's Road

I remember the day I got my first credit card. It was 1992. I was 21. My mother and I were sitting in the office of a credit union. She was co-signing for me, so that I could have a credit card to take with me on a trip to Ireland and England later that year. I was given a credit limit of $500! In 1992, that was a large sum of money for a 21 year-old. That's equivalent to $2,500 in today's dollars.

I was supposed to use this card for emergencies only. Yeah right! What neither my mom nor I realized was that this was my first step on the long, winding road into credit card hell.

I returned from Ireland and England having had an amazing time. I had tons of pictures and $400 worth of debt to prove it. The trip was soon a memory of the past. My debt was something that came with a monthly reminder that I ignored. I would pay the minimum, but nothing more.

I should share with you that my parents, similar to most, didn't provide me with much financial education. Sure, they instructed me to be frugal and warned me about spending too much. They never helped me, though, to really understand how money and credit work. I don't fault them. Most of us don't learn money management while growing up - not from our families nor school. I'll continue with my story...

When I was back in the States and working again, my credit card spending became a bit of a habit. I would make purchases with my card and pay the monthly minimum, always maintaining a balance near my credit limit. I didn't really understand the impact my credit card was having on me and my credit score, or even how much interest I was paying.

Then the first increase in my credit limit came. I was shocked! It felt like getting a raise. I look at it differently now, but back then I thought it was great to be able to spend $1,000. That's exactly what I did. I now had an extra $500. This was before the Internet and online shopping. Back then, we had catalogs. Over the phone I ordered the bright and shiny things I saw in catalogs and had them shipped to me. It was all so exciting!

Eventually I moved from Colorado to South Dakota. While living in South Dakota, I made a pretty meager income. I relied heavily on my credit cards to keep me afloat. I remember writing checks for a couple of dollars at a time to make minimum payments. At this time, I was regularly behind and being charged late fees. It wasn't sinking in that I was spending more than I was making or that it mattered. I was financially weak and credit cards were my financial crutch.

I remember one time I was in a pinch and my parents deposited $300 into my checking account. I thanked them, and then headed to the bank to withdraw it. It was already gone, though! Where was it? Had I been robbed? Someone stole my money, the money I really (not really) needed. No one robbed me. Someone smarter and more responsible (a computer, in fact) decided that it was better I pay the well-past-due balance on my credit card before I did anything else with it.

In reality, that computer was smarter than I was at the time - and for much longer. After moving back to Colorado, I got a full time job, a "real" job, and was making quite a bit more money. That solved everything, right? Wrong! I kept spending and charging and the credit card companies kept raising my credit limit. Hell, they're not stupid. I was a cash cow for them. I was paying hundreds of dollars a year in late fees and finance charges. Why cut off a good source of revenue?

Fast forward eight years with the same chicanery to 2004. John and I were sharing a two-bedroom basement apartment (our landlord preferred to call it a "garden-level walk-in"). I was driving a beat up, ten year-old car. I had a closet full of old clothes and $17,000 of credit card debt. I was recently laid off of work and expecting $21,000 in severance. Halleluiah!

I could've used that smarter computer again. Instead of saving my severance money and quickly finding a new job, I took the summer off and blew through most of that money, while still making minimum credit card payments.

When I finally started looking for a new job, I was $14,000 in debt. John and I had $51,000 in combined debt. We were a total mess when it came to finances and both worked in financial services. It was at that point that we realized something needed to change.

John's Road

Before I moved to Colorado, I received $5,000 as a gift from my grandparents. I just finished college the previous spring, and I was starting my life. This $5,000 made me rich, or so I thought. My roommate, a friend from college, and I found an apartment not far from Denver but close enough to the mountains for snowboarding and skiing. I thought I was supposed to be a grownup at this point in my life. Grownups don't hang posters on their walls with sticky tack. Grownups don't turn makeshift crates into shelves. Grownups don't sleep on futons. Grownups have a brand new queen-sized bed. They have new Pottery Barn furniture. They have framed artwork on their walls, new pots and pans and dishes – and lots of other new and expensive things.

As you can imagine, I burned through that $5,000 quickly. But, don't worry. I was okay. I had a credit card. I would put a bit on here and a bit on there. The whole time, I felt as though I had a fortune in the bank, especially when I only had to make the minimum payment to my credit card each month.

Don't forget that I was new to Colorado, home to some of the best snowboarding in the world. Obviously, I needed new boarding equipment and mountain passes. Before long, I had over $30,000 in credit card debt! Yes, that is the price of a pretty decent car (brand new) or a down payment on a home - or I could've put myself through college again.

But let me add to the details because our goal is to show you how David and I acquired our debt differently, all with the hope that you'll relate to one of our stories. This will help you see yourself in us and show you that there is a better way of living than drowning in debt. I built up most of my debt with big ticket purchases. When I first moved to Colorado, I immediately bought the things that I thought I needed to make me feel like an adult.

I first bought a $1,000 bed, including a new down comforter and bedding, along with sheets, pillows, duvet and the rest, all from Pottery Barn. I needed to have a Michelangelo print that I received for my birthday framed for $300. I bought a brand new couch from Pottery Barn, as mentioned above, for $3,000. I needed a new TV for $800. What goes best with a new TV? A new TV stand, of course! Actually, I bought a Spanish-style armoire for $500. Then, I spent $1,500 on two Pottery Barn coffee tables. Like I said, I needed new snowboarding equipment: new board, boots, binding, pants, helmet, jacket, socks, gloves and more - costing about $2,000, all combined.

At this time of my life, I was going out to clubs on a weekly basis, if not more, to meet new people and make friends. Of course, I needed new designer clothes each weekend, at the very least. I'm talking head-to-toe new. My addiction was the Great Italian Clothier, Diesel. Jeans alone cost $250, minimum. Let's figure I was spending somewhere upwards of $300 to $500 each week on a new outfit. For your information, I am not actually a celebrity, but I certainly spent like one.

It took me seven years to pay these debts off. That is seven *long* years, which might have been longer had I not decided to own my mistakes and work to put them behind me. I made many mistakes along the way. We hope to spare you those mistakes.

One such mistake, which has paid off in the long run, was enrolling in (and graduating from) graduate school. Getting my masters was something I always wanted to do and figured I would do eventually. However, the catalyst for me doing this sooner than planned was that my employer reimbursed me up to $5,000 annually for additional education. I thought I would use this total of $10,000 over the two years it would take to finish school and put it towards my debt. Big mistake! Huge! Since what happens in Vegas stays in Vegas, all I will say is that I had an excellent time in Vegas (said Bill & Ted style).

Fast forward a few years when David and I found ourselves living in a friend's basement in downtown Denver. Originally, we moved in together to split expenses and because it was a sweet location. It wasn't long after we moved in that we had the awakening. Here we were, two 30-something men, both of whom work in financial services and should know better, living paycheck to paycheck, in debt up to our eyeballs. Living in a basement wasn't our definition of success.

Roads Merge

About late 2005, our "debt roads" merged. This happened when we started talking honestly about our finances. It was because of these honest conversations that we started having clarity. Between the two of us, we had about $51,000 in debt. This was equivalent to two new cars, an awesome down payment on a house, or a boat load of money to start our retirement nest eggs.

What really hit home for us was our living situation. We were making decent money in financial services, but sharing a two-bedroom *basement* apartment. We aren't talking a place in cities like New York, San Fran, or Boston. This was Denver, where you could still rent an apartment for less than a thousand dollars a month. By the way, for this apartment we paid less than a thousand for everything, and we mean *everything*: rent, satellite TV, TIVO, electricity, Internet, everything! Where was our money going?

We came up with a plan. We did some analysis, decided what to do and how to do it and the rest is history. Two-and-a-half years later, we were both free of our credit card debt. But don't get us wrong.

It wasn't easy. It was painful at times, humbling at others, and frustrating throughout.

You cannot imagine how we felt when it was all over, though. We triumphed! We did it! We want you to have the same feeling of accomplishment. You'll go through ups and downs in the process, but you'll reach the same end. Overcome your debt, reap the rewards - and turn your life around!

Chapter Two:

A Foundation of Debt

History of Debt

Let's begin with a history lesson. Okay, we know, not everyone's favorite subject. We think this brief bit of history is valuable, though, as most of us are credit card era kids who've never lived in a world without them. It's quite interesting and will show you that, although debt is not new, it has become a bigger and bigger aspect of our lives - and thus, has the potential to become more and more of a problem if not used cautiously.

Although it may seem that credit is a modern convenience, this simply isn't true. It may be that the magnitude of the problem is new, but debt has been around for centuries.

Historians have traced the first use of "credit" back to ancient Assyria, Babylon, and Egypt some 3,000 years ago. The system used at that time was much more archaic than our more "evolved" system of today. If you want to put a positive spin on it, there's a lot less loss of life for those who default on loans today.

Credit cards started being used in the United States before World War I and were, in fact, dog tags rather than the plastic version we have come to know and love. The modern version of the credit card was introduced in the 1950's by Francis McNamara. McNamara capitalized on the need for traveling salesmen to pay restaurants without the risk of carrying loads of cash. Being a businessman himself, he saw the benefit of earning a modest return on the money he temporarily loaned to his credit card holders. Abracadabra, *Diners Club* was born! Initially, the Diners Club was used only in restaurants; hence the name, but he eventually expanded it to gas stations, hotels, airlines, and so on.

Not to be outdone, Bank of America created the BankAmericard in 1951, which eventually became Visa. It wasn't until the 1960's that banks and credit card agencies started the onslaught of advertising and mailbox stuffing.

In 2011, the average credit-carrying American household had credit card debt of more than $15,956. Divide that by all adult Americans, and each had more than $3,700 in credit card debt. No doubt this has only increased since the housing crisis and rising gas and food prices. Many people own cars and homes they simply cannot afford and are at risk of losing them or have had them repossessed. SUVs and homes are depreciating in value and, ultimately, becoming a loss that owners can't unload.

Much like its constituents, our government isn't doing better. The U.S. government is tallying up a deficit that's not worth quoting because it will be billions if not trillions more by the time this book goes to print. Our country is borrowing from other countries to subsidize our lifestyle. We are a country addicted to - and drowning in - debt. We believe we must all take ownership of our mistakes. We aren't making excuses, but it's somewhat understandable why many of us find ourselves buried with debt. Everyone's doing it. Why not us? We are building a deficit that will take decades to pay off. This leads us to the history of mortgages.

The history of home loans or mortgages was much different than credit cards. Before the 1920's, those who had land would lend the use of their land to others, usually farmers, with the borrower assuming the obligation of making regular payments to the lender without necessarily indicating any terms and conditions or providing the borrower with many rights. This meant that the lender could refuse payment, repossess the land at any time without reason, or increase the amount due without restriction. These were private transactions that included no government or professional agency.

Because of the potential for abuse, the government got involved with mortgage lending via The Federal Housing Association (FHA). The mortgage as we know it today, however, didn't start to take shape until the 1930's when the government saw potential to help pull the U.S. out of the Great Depression. This was part of FDR's New Deal.

There's a theory that this government intervention may have prolonged the Great Depression. At that time, though, mortgage loan terms were limited to fifty percent of the property's market value with a term typically between three to five years.[1]

That's right, 50% down and only three to five year loans! Only about 40% of Americans owned their own home. Due to increased flexibility with FHA loans from numerous programs, including LBJ's Great Society, the percentage of homeowners is over 70% today, with terms increasing to the standard 30 years and, in some markets, 50 years.

Identifiable Characteristics

Let's face it; if you're under the age of 80, your life has been a part of the debt culture. It's all around us. Think about it. Can you avoid debt? Ask yourself. Better yet, we will ask you. Our experience tells us that if you answer yes to one or more of the following questions you're a likely candidate for overspending and thus susceptible to acquiring debt. Be honest with your answers.

1. Am I a person who loves to spend and often buys on impulse?
2. Am I a person who has been pre-approved by a credit card company and taken advantage of it?
3. Do I need to have the latest technology or designer clothes?
4. Do I find myself browsing the mall or online stores without a specific item or even a need in mind?

5. Do I feel guilty or depressed that my neighbor, friend or co-worker has nicer things than me?
6. Is it difficult for me to separate my needs from my wants?
7. Do I often find myself saying I will pay off my debts later?
8. Do I often find myself saying I will save money later?
9. Am I without emergency savings or liquid cash to fall back on in a financial pinch?
10. Am I surrounded by people who must always have the best of everything?
11. Am I living paycheck to paycheck?
12. Do I have a pulse?

The fascinating aspect with credit cards specifically (and debt in general) is that it affects every income bracket, every class, race, creed, and orientation. Uncontrollable credit card debt affects the college student out on her own for the first time. Enormous mortgages bury the young newlyweds trying to start a life together. Older, established women and men are hounded by credit card and other loan agencies because of their late payments. Even the elderly are borrowing money against the value of their homes so they can afford healthcare and to live day to day. (This phenomenon is termed a "reverse mortgage.")

Amazingly, issues with debt affect multi-millionaires! In fact, the more you have or the more you make only increases the amount you can borrow and the deeper the hole you can dig for yourself. Remember David's story about getting an increase on his spending limit? Just think about the line of credit people like Bill Gates, Paris Hilton, or Shaquille O'Neil have. A real life and tragic example of this was Michael Jackson. Aside from his other issues, he was a financial nightmare. If you're trying to keep up with Mr. Jones who earns three times what you do and is the president of a successful tech company, just know that his income and position may help him to build up three times your *debt* and three times your *stress*.

At this point, you need to recognize two simple facts. First, you are not immune from the temptations that cause debt. We all can be, and probably have been, tempted by debt - or at least the lifestyle that debt can seemingly bring us. Secondly, if you succumb to debt, you're going to be plagued by the burden debt brings.

With all this said, it's only natural to want a decent standard of living. We all do, but needing and wanting and *wanting right now* are three very different things. It is the desire to have *right now* - and the succumbing to that desire - that has buried so many. Our instant gratification society makes every single one of us susceptible to being overcome with debt.

Two principles in this book: Living Below Your Means and Cash is King, address these problems. This doesn't just apply to small purchases, either. Think about the mortgage crisis of 2008, which lead to the financial crisis that began in 2009 and continues today. It was primarily brought on by the insatiable desire of millions to have a bigger, nicer home to show off, combined with the malicious methods of mortgage brokers and lenders who were raking in fees and commissions on sub-prime and designer loans.

In many ways, it all comes down to greed. We are not preaching about greed, that's what the Bible is for. However, know that there is a subtle thread of greed that runs through all the reasons why many of us are where we are financially.

Unfortunately, one of our government's solutions to correcting the housing crisis was to give each person a $600 tax rebate with the hope that we buy more stuff. That's right! What does a government on the verge of bankruptcy do to help us quit the addiction of spending beyond our financially-bankrupt means? It enables us by giving us more spending money. Keep in mind that with the first Bush tax rebate in 2001, barely 1/3 of those who received that $300 saved it. The rest spent it, which was the government's intent - to stimulate the economy. The question is how many spent only $300 and no more?

Statistics of Debt and Its Effect on the Individual

At this point, you understand how debt was originally created and what its intended purpose was (to make someone else rich). In addition, you know that you and pretty much everyone you know is susceptible to building up too much debt. That being the case, the principles in this book are valuable to everyone. You may want to encourage others to read this book after you do, or even give it as a gift to someone you know with a debt problem. Before we begin discussing the principles, let's take a look at why debt can be such a financial death-blow to so many. How do debt and the debt industry impact us?

Keep in mind that not all of us are influenced by these statistics, but consider the impact they may have on you or your spouse, children, parents, and friends - and your relationship with each of them.

Consider these facts compiled by Mark Brinker at www.hoffmanbrinker.com and a tragedy that made international news. As you go through the list, you'll see some of the emotions we experienced while we were going through this in our own lives. We're confident that you will feel similarly.

- The national average default rate as of January, 2010 stood at 27.88% and the mean default rate is 28.99%[2] (*Stress, lying, sleeplessness, and depression*)
- According to Fitch Ratings, the number of credit card defaults hit a level of 11.37%, the highest level since a record of 11.52% in September, 2009[3] (*Again, stress and more stress!*)
- U.S. households received approximately 5.3 billion, yes, that is *billion*, offers for new credit cards in 2007 (*Compelled to spend, we open new cards to be able to maintain a lifestyle and dupe ourselves into thinking we must be okay financially if we're pre-approved*)

- The average interest rate for standard bank credit cards topped 13.67% as of November, 2010 *(Stress, doubt and fear of never being able to pay it off)*
- Regarding college students and their use of credit cards:
  - Half of college undergrads had four or more credit cards in 2008, up 43% from 2004 and 32% from 2000 *(Freedom, but no responsibility)*
- As of March, 2011, the average credit card debt per household with such debt was more than $15,956 *(Stress, sadness, a feeling of no way out)*
- In August, 2008, a mother in Massachusetts committed suicide because she and her family faced foreclosure on their home. Her hope was that the life insurance money she presumed her husband would collect would be used to pay off their mortgage, and she felt her family would be better off without her if that was the way to get rid of their debt *(Hopelessness, pain, and depression)*

As some of our comments show, being burdened with debt can seem lonely and make you feel as if you're an isolated case. You are not! You may feel that it is because you don't make enough money. It is not! It may seem as though you are financially immature. You are! That's right; we just said you are financially immature. You may think you are being taken by clever marketing and confusing credit and finance rules and regulations. You are! But again, you're not alone. You've lost control, millions have and it is time to take it back.

It's almost as if we're born into this world believing we need a credit card and that we must use it. What we find most frustrating is the aggressive marketing tactics credit card companies use towards college students. We believe in a free and open market. However, the problem is that cash-strapped and financially unprepared students are assaulted by advertisements to sign up for credit cards, but not nearly half as much attention is given to educate them about credit cards, money management, and investing. Why do we spend so much time, money and resources preparing these young adults to earn as much money as possible and not about money, how it works, and how they can make it work for them?

There's no doubt why credit card companies target college students. Though there are colleges that ban marketing of credit cards, it doesn't necessarily mean marketing to these students isn't happening. With the Internet, TV, text messaging, Facebook, Twitter, etc., a company is not constrained to putting an advertising table at the student cafeteria or mailing a flyer to a dormitory mailbox anymore.

Not only is this an easy population to target, if a credit card company can start you off early, they'll likely have you for life. What these companies know is that college students pay even less attention to the small print of their credit card agreements and review their monthly statements less than working adults do. We know we were more concerned about our next keg party than our credit card agreement and statement. Many aren't aware that their "historically low introductory rate" can very quickly skyrocket well before the offer says it will under certain conditions. This is a great way of forcing you to become a "member for life."

The other secret these companies mislead you into believing is that they want you to make your payments on time. The reality is that they make a whole lot more if you don't. They charge you compounding interest on your balance and excessive fees if you miss or are even just a little bit late on your monthly payments. This means, that even if you stop making purchases on your card, your debt continues to grow until the balance is paid in full. This is a nice way to start a career. You need a six-figure salary to pay off all your student loans and credit card debt.

We need to mention here again that we are not against a free and open market and we only cautiously accept government regulations of any kind when it comes to business. Credit card companies provide a service that many people want, and they have ingenious marketing to make that service even more appealing to the masses. Consequently, they are benefiting from ever-increasing revenue and growth. Our goal is not to ask for government intervention or to force credit card companies to change their business model. Our goal is to simply provide you, our reader, with the knowledge of how credit cards work and to provide strategies for pulling you out of debt.

Chapter Three:

The Inspiration to Get Out of Debt

You Can Become Debt Free

Now that you're demoralized and feeling like your problem is insurmountable, we have great news. It's NOT! You can pay off all your debt. You don't need to resort to bankruptcy; you do not need to call in an attorney to have the debt written down so that you only have to pay a fraction of it. What would you really learn if this is how your problem is fixed, anyway?

The reality is that there are millions of people every day working hard to pay off their debt. They're working to live the life they can afford. True, there are fewer of them than in the past, but we are out there. And guess what? We are the ones who are going to be financially successful. We are going to have really enjoyed our lives and not necessarily all the stupid junk we bought. We are going to understand and be able to help others. Wouldn't you love to be the first one in your family to teach your children what money really means, help your family get on the right path, and not be buried by debt? Think of the advantages your children will have if they never have to make an interest payment in their lives.

As can be seen from our own stories, we both made horrible financial mistakes that put us in a gross amount of debt. However, despite what seemed at times to be insurmountable odds, we were able to overcome them. If you can see yourself in either of us at our lowest points, you should certainly be able to see yourself in us at our best. Your situation will likely have its uniqueness, but the basics are the same.

We never want to go back to the agonizing and depressing lifestyle that debt brought us. Been there! When you are in debt, it is always in the back of your mind. Every time you pay a bill or make a purchase, you think about your debt. Will you have enough to pay it off? What other bills do you have to pay? Can you afford to pay the rent this month? What about the phone, the electricity, or groceries? Every time you get a bill in the mail, the thought of your debt comes to mind. The bill collector is calling, the kids want more, and you forgot to pay the phone bill. The car needs new brakes; the dishwasher is on the fritz. Ahhhh! This is not the way you want to live your life. You only get one – at least, most of us do, Shirley McLaine!

Debt is suffocating. Debt holds you back and pushes you down. Debt prevents you from living the life you want to live. It keeps you from comfortably doing the things you want to do. It prevents you from preparing for your future, let alone the here and now.

What are you waiting for? The debt that weighs you down can be lifted off your shoulders. The reality is that with a little time, determination, and understanding and the principles we present in this book, you too can be debt free and on your way to financial victory. Hearing our stories should help you see the opportunities that lay before you.

The very reason we wrote this book is because we've been through it. Having been there, we can provide you with effective guidance and support to achieve your financial goals. You can learn from our mistakes and achieve your own positive cash flow more quickly and with fewer errors.

At this point, you must ask yourself a few questions. "Am I committed to becoming debt-free?" "Am I ready to do what it takes to achieve financial success?" "Am I tired of the negative feeling carrying this debt causes?" "Am I prepared for the tough, but achievable fight ahead of me?"

If you answered "yes" to these questions, you're already on your way to financial freedom. If you believe in your heart that you are ready to do what it takes to become debt free, you've already made the first step. If you believe you can attain your goal, then you have nothing to lose. Get started today!

We Can All Live Debt Free

The next step is to learn what it takes to become debt free. There are millions of people who have worked hard to pay down their debt. They may have spent extra hours at work, taken out equity in their home, maybe consolidated and/or gone through bankruptcy, or they've made minor changes to their lifestyle, so that they could achieve the goal of being debt free. Sadly, many have given up, drifted back to old habits. They may have gone out and rewarded themselves for their efforts, only to pile it up all over again.

One of the biggest lessons of becoming debt free is living the principles of a *debt free life!* We will teach you this. Although it's not intuitive, living debt free means you will have more money than ever and you can enjoy a much better quality of life. By using the tools in this book, not only will you be able to climb out of debt, but you'll continue to stay debt free.

The Rewards of Being Debt Free

There are many rewards that come with living debt-free. We just mentioned one - a better lifestyle. Before we elaborate, let's do some visualizing. Close your eyes and contemplate the feelings of financial freedom. Consider the feelings you'll have and the stress that will wash away. Consider the pride you'll have in your accomplishment, how your mental state will shift, how you'll look and sound. Focus on the life you'll live. Think of the person you'll be. Okay, Marsha Brady, maybe you won't look like a teen model, but you'll certainly feel like one.

Consider this new you for a few minutes and, in the space below, write down five feelings you'll have.

Focus on the positive rather than the negative emotions that will be yours.

1.
2.
3.
4.
5.

Now that you understand your emotions, let's take a moment to think about what you'll do with this new life. What is it you really want to achieve in life? What goals and aspirations do you have? Are you hoping to be more philanthropic? Do you want to buy your first home or an investment property? Do you want to retire early? Do you want to invest in your children through school? Do you want to go back to school yourself? Do you want to have a rainy-day fund? Do you want to invest? Don't focus on things, but think of financial capabilities - like investing, personal growth and helping others.

In the space below, write down five things you want to do or accomplish when you are debt free.

1.
2.
3.
4.
5.

Reflect now on all these tangible and intangible desires of yours and consider that when you're debt free, you'll be able to attain these goals. When you're debt free and you become financially mature, you'll be able to take those vacations, buy those shoes, or give more to charity - all without the burden of debt lingering over your head. You'll be able to do these things with the freedom of knowing that you're financially capable. You'll be able to truly enjoy the things you have, instead of your things bringing you stress.

This is what you deserve; this is what your family and friends deserve. You'll be able to live in the present and be fully engaged with your loved ones. Live the life you are meant to live. Eliminate your debt and enjoy the financial freedom that you just penned for yourself above and have that "I am better than a teen model" feeling!

Chapter Four:

The Commitment
to Become Debt Free

Understanding What It Will Take to Become Debt Free

Let's consider what it will take for you to become debt free. You now understand a little about debt, its history, and its impact on people, including yourself. You also understand that you, like others, can achieve a debt free life. You can correct your current course and set a new one for a brighter future. Below are a few points you should know before proceeding with your plan of eliminating your debt.

First, it's important to keep yourself from wanting to give up. Remember how you got here and understand that becoming debt free *will not happen overnight*. Some of you took many years to get yourselves to where you are today. For some, you got into this situation rather quickly because a dramatic, once-in-a-lifetime event. Either way, going into this process with the understanding that it will take months or years, to eliminate will help reduce future frustration. Keep in mind that it is possible. You can do this! It took us over two years of hard work. It's going to be hard, but boy will it be worth it.

Second, this is going to require some drastic changes on your part. The hardest step for most is cutting up all credit cards. From this point forward, you will no longer be able to rely on credit cards for any purchases. You can't have them in your wallet, in your purse, anywhere accessible - not even in a frozen block of ice in the freezer. You must learn to rely *only* on the money you make. What!? Huh?! We must be crazy!

Though this may sound radical and even impossible, this step is the surest and quickest way to eliminate debt. Through our individual journeys to becoming debt free, John cut up his cards and no longer relied on them for anything. David kept his around "in case of an emergency." Though he started with more debt, John was able to pay off his credit card over a year sooner than David because he didn't keep his card around for an "emergency."

The idea here is to get out of debt as quickly as possible because the longer you are paying off debt, the longer you are preventing yourself from investing and making your money work for you (i.e., saving for your future). Chew on this one for a bit, we have plenty of other suggestions.

The third point to keep in mind is that you will have to look at spending differently. You will have to adjust your social life a little - and in some cases, a lot! You will need to become more aware of where your money is coming and going.

Lastly, like an athlete, you must make the target the goal and know that your financial goals are attainable. You must focus on the good feeling of no longer having to make monthly payments to a credit card company. Focus on how you're going to feel when you're putting the money you used to put towards your debt towards your investments or towards saving up for an all-cash, paid vacation. Both of us enjoy not being a part of statistical averages. The average American has thousands of dollars of credit card debt and that's a party to which we don't want an invitation.

The Lifestyle

No matter what your income bracket, race, creed, etc., you must be honest with yourself. You must shed your old skin and put on a new one. (No, this book won't make you look younger. For that you will just have to live with the fact that you spent too much time in the sun as a kid.) Let others know that you're making some personal lifestyle changes. We hope that most of these changes will be permanent. They will become your *new* lifestyle, but you will also come to enjoy an even *better* life because of them.

Remember that the only way to break the cycle of ever-increasing debt is to no longer acquire debt and to use all available resources to pay down your debt quickly. This may mean (GASP!) being frugal. It's time to stop joining the crowd for happy hour every Friday night. You don't need the latest Coach purse or the newest iPad. (Come on, Apple! We know you can give us all the memory we need now and not force us to buy new products every year!) And, from now on, you can only take that extravagant vacation once you've saved for it.

With all this in mind, know that you'll be reaching your goals sooner than you can imagine. We certainly don't expect everyone to be hermits or wear socks with holes. Later we'll discuss how to have fun while not spending everything you earn. All we're asking is that you start *being honest with yourself* and be willing to make some sacrifices. There's a good chance you got to where you are by not being truthful about your financial situation. Now's the time to be real, not boring. Come on! You can tell we're not boring, right? We understand that it's impossible to stay home every night, so we won't ask - not that we want to ask.

As we mentioned, we partied quite a bit and neither of us regret it. We also lived well above our means. It was fun, but it became a burden, and we had to start being honest. We made a paradigm shift. It was tough, but worth it. We're examples of those who have done it - and, that being the case - you can too! We're now examples of those who are relieved that we're not carrying a credit card balance.

We have to be honest, though admittedly dorky. We managed to have a good time with this. Each week we went grocery shopping (we will provide you with some great tips), we tried to beat the previous week's percentage of savings. It's a real hoot to save 50% - and even 60% - of the grocery bill total. The fact that we use the word "hoot" tells you how dorky we are.

We found a number of things to do at home or in town cheaply - or even free - such as dining, seeing a movie, and visiting a museum. There are plenty of ways to have fun and save 50% or more - you just have to be willing to ask for it. Another recommended book purchase of ours is *The Entertainment Book*. We'll discuss this in detail later. For now, check out www.entertainment.com. You may also want to join *Groupon, Living Social,* and *Amazon Local.* Remember to not get caught up in buying just because there's a deal. But when possible; add it to your debt payment plan.

Having a Support System

Having a strong support system is important. The nice thing about a support system is that the first step after becoming honest with yourself is being honest with others. This is an integral step. We suggest talking with friends and family about your goals and what you're planning on doing to attain them. We found that many of our friends and family were in similar situations. The statistics support this. We found that our attempt at paying off our debt motivated others to do the same. So, when you're thinking of what you want to do some random Saturday night, invite people with the same financial goals over for a movie or a game night.

We don't mean that everyone in your life has a mound of debt, but most everyone has one or more financial goals that would be more easily attained by pulling in the financial reigns a little. You can be the leader in your circle of influence (*7 Habits of Highly Effective People*).

Creating a support system provides you with more than just friends. When you verbalize your goals, your friends and family will understand your boundaries. For example, if the old you would regularly go out for a fancy dinner, followed by a movie or a play, your friends won't be upset when you cut back. If you frequently shopped with a friend as "therapy," she won't be offended when you stop joining in the therapy because you let her know your situation in advance. If you let her know your plans, she will be more understanding. She may even find other "therapeutic" activities that are *not so expensive* (NSE).

This brings us to our next point. By letting loved ones know your goals, they'll be able to provide you with advice and support. Although we, the authors of this book, think we have all the answers, there's a good chance we don't. (If you tell anyone, we'll deny that we EVER said that!) Really, the best part of including others is the support they can provide. Support is what you need in the weak moments. Not only will they provide support, but they will check up on you, ask about your progress, and champion your personal cause.

A final benefit of letting others know your goals is that it simply feels good being honest. You will feel relieved by not having to keep up with those damn Jones' anymore. They're not even nice people and the wife has split ends! *Hey, we said we'd help you become debt free, not get you into heaven.*

Let's get started! Next is the commitment contract. Yes, a contract. We think this is important because it puts your commitment in writing, is tangible, and requires a witness. You may not want to tell everyone what you're doing, but you have to tell at least one person. Choose someone who will be supportive. Read through the contract, fill in the information, and sign your commitment to yourself.

Commitment Contract to Financial Freedom

I, _____, admit that I have been misleading myself and potentially others by living above my means and accumulating an unhealthy amount of personal debt. Because I acknowledge this, I fully commit to stop using my credit cards and accessing other forms of debt to maintain this inflated lifestyle. From now on, I will live on the true money that I earn and will aggressively work towards paying off my debt and loans as quickly as possible with the intention of never accumulating them again. I make this commitment to myself, my family, and my loved ones so that I can live my best life.

I agree to create and follow a plan based on the principles outlined in *4: The Four Principles of a Debt Free Life* so that I can be debt free. It is my goal to pay off all my credit card and personal loan debt, by _____, 20XX.

_____
Signature   Date

_____
Witness/Partner/Sponsor   Date

Chapter Five:

Principle One:
Be Money Conscious

Introduction to the Money Consciousness Principle

Has there ever been a time when you went through an intersection and thought to yourself, "Was that a green light?" That is being *unconscious*.

Most people are this way when it comes to their money. Most don't know how much they really earn, where their money goes, and what they can afford. Most don't know these facts because they choose not to know them. It's a defense mechanism. If you know, then you have to live accordingly. With a little courage, you can learn about your finances and turn a negative situation into a positive one. In so doing, you'll be able to achieve the financial success you want. In the following chapter, we'll walk you through a step-by-step analysis of how much you earn, where your money comes from, where it's going, and discuss how you can most effectively manage your money to meet short-term and long-term goals.

The importance of being money conscious, if only about your own financial situation, cannot be overstated. If knowledge is power, then financial knowledge is the engine to your financial success. Though some achieve financial security while being unconscious, most won't. This is why Being Money Conscious is the first principle of achieving financial freedom. It's the foundation to the other three principles. Surprisingly, mastering this principle will put you light years ahead of most when it comes to understanding money and its effect on your life.

Understanding the Value of Your Dollar

What's a dollar? A dollar is a piece of paper not even worth the cost it takes to make. Money is a means to measure the value of a product or service. By its simplest definition, a dollar is a monetary unit of measurement. When making a purchase, you must be conscious of how much your money is worth to you, and likewise, your perceived value of the item you're purchasing.

The answers to the following questions help quantify the value of your dollar. What is your dollar worth? How long and hard did you have to work to earn that dollar? Is it worth the same to you as it is to someone else? Is a product or service worth as much as the asking price? Will your dollar be worth the same tomorrow as it is today? Will that product or service be worth the same tomorrow as it is today?

Let's look closely at the first question; what's your dollar worth to you? The easiest way to quantify this is to calculate how much you earn per hour. This is easy to do. For the time being, let's forget we have to pay taxes. If you're paid hourly, your hourly wage is the figure you should use. If you're paid a salary, you should take the annual total (gross salary) and divide that number by 2,000. Two thousand is the number of hours you are paid to work per year. Of course, this may be different than the actual number of hours you work. If you're paid minimum wage, the federal minimum wage for non-exempt employees has been $7.25 since 2009. This can vary at the state level. For example, based off of a 40-hour work week, if you make $50,000 annually, you make $25 per hour. If you make a million a year, you're bringing in a cool $500 an hour. Nice, huh? What does this mean? What can you buy with $7.25, or $25 or $500? What can you buy with one hour's worth of work? There's a pretty big disparity among those three wages.

Let's look at this in a different way. On her *Favorite Things* shows, Oprah (You remember Oprah don't you?) used to talk about $80 tins of popcorn because they were sooo fabulous! What does that mean for someone who makes $22,000 per year? What does it mean for a person who's making $50,000 per year, and what does that mean for Oprah? If you make $22,000 a year, you need to work about 7.25 hours before taxes to be able to buy that earth-shattering tin of popcorn. If you're making $50,000 a year, you need to work slightly over three hours – and for Oprah, she earns more than that before getting out of bed. The reality is that your dollar means something completely different to you than it does to someone making $22,000 or to someone like Oprah Winfrey. Of course, there aren't many "someone's" like Oprah Winfrey.

Yes, there are necessities. You need a roof over your head, you need transportation, you need to eat and you need clothing. Beyond these basics, you can spend your money how you want. This extra money is your disposable income. The kind of roof over your head and the kind of roof over Bill Gates' head, however, are very different because he has much more disposable income than you do. The less you make the less disposable income you have.

Another way of looking at this is by assessing what percentage of your take home pay you spend on necessities. We often forget this when we see how celebrities live and we try to "buy" into their lifestyle. Angelina Jolie can go on a shopping spree at Hermes and it will impact a much smaller percentage of her income and net worth than it would you. This is why you should've dropped out of college and become a movie star. We're joking, of course, unless your parents are already movie stars like Ms. Jolie-Pitt's. This buyers-envy, as we call it, inevitably leads to financial disaster, even for Uncle Sam.

The question, then, is can you really afford what you're buying? We've all gotten caught up with the idea that "I deserve it," "I work hard; I should get what I want." True, you may work hard and you may feel that you deserve it, but can you afford it?

After we were together for a little over a year, we felt that because we were working so hard and we had not gone on vacation together, we "deserved" a trip to Miami. A Miami vacation is not necessarily a bad thing, except when you don't have the cash to pay for it. We spent $3,000 on a vacation that we mostly put on credit cards. Does that make sense?

Here's another example. Let's go shopping. We have two friends with us: our good buddy, the million-dollar real estate broker and our sassy and fun friend who's a waitress at the corner diner. You're an average middle income worker – no frills, but not broke. You each need a car.

Off you go to the dealership. You all decide you want new BMWs. You walk into the dealership and there sits a beautiful, black 7 Series at $85,000. Is the cost of that BMW the same to the broker, to you, and to the waitress? The broker can buy one. His earnings can support a car like this, it fits his lifestyle, and he can pay it off in about a month. For you, you can get it if you stretch yourself. Even with $5,994 cash due at signing, your payments will be $769 per month for a 36 month lease. Considering your true financial goals, is this the best place to put $800 a month? Finally, for the waitress, this purchase is a definite no! There isn't a bank in the U.S. that should finance her for an $85,000 car.

The reality is that all three of you, in this example, want the BMW 7 Series. They're great looking cars and are reliable, plus you all work hard and deserve it. Right? Whether or not you all deserve it, you shouldn't all buy it because some of you cannot afford it.

The easiest way to tell if someone is financially unconscious is if they have something they simply cannot afford. A perfect, real life example of this is when David met a guy in L.A. who had a brand new BMW 3 Series, but was living in a two bedroom apartment with three people. The way to become financially *conscious* is to start recognizing and buying what you can afford. Love the life you can afford, or you will not love the life you live.

The point is that the value of a dollar is relative. It's relative to how much you earn and how much you've saved. What's even more relative is the value of a product or service. Just because a store is asking a certain price for a product you may want to buy doesn't mean that's what it is worth. The very next day the same store may take 50% off their asking price. Another brand of the same product may have a lower asking price based on the difference in name.

When we cut back our spending, we started purchasing store brand products, such as body wash, shampoo, conditioner, etc. It was amazing to us - and we're not really sure why – to learn these products were no different than the name-brands we previously couldn't live without. True they may smell prettier, but they do the same job.

These are factors to consider when making purchases. You need to be aware of inflated asking prices, but also conscious of how much your money is worth to you. Likewise, you need to be aware of other factors that impact prices.

Economists like to track the value of eggs over time to demonstrate the value of a dollar. This is because throughout history, eggs have been a staple of the human diet. In 1960, a dozen eggs cost the consumer $0.57. By 1980, they almost doubled to $0.93. In 2000, those same eggs cost $1.89. Today they cost up to $3.46. *(Obtained from the U.S. Dept. of Agriculture and the California Dept. of Food and Agriculture)*

What we have just described is called "inflation." Inflation is the *depreciating* value of the dollar or the *appreciating* cost of goods or services over time. You must earn more today than you did ten years ago to maintain the same standard of living (or to buy those same eggs). A couple of ways a person who is money conscious maintains or increases their standard of living is by saving and putting money in investments that earn more than the rate of inflation.

Other factors to be conscious of relative to cost are local, state, and federal taxes. If you're buying a product from somewhere else in the world, there are costs of transportation. Weather has a great impact on costs, especially on food, both with growing food and transporting it. The supply and the demand of a product or service will have an impact, just as our relations with other countries with whom we import and export goods. This may sound dry, but it's all related to the cost of goods and services you buy, and you should have a fundamental understanding of how it impacts you.

In summary, the value of a dollar to you is not the same as the value of a dollar to someone else. It's related primarily to how much you make and secondarily to the product you want or need. Before making any purchase, especially for things that aren't needs, it's wise to assess the true cost of that product or service and compare that to how much disposable income you have. How long or hard did you have to work in order to make the purchase? Does it make sense to buy it now at today's price or wait until later?

Knowing How Much Money You Really Make

Now that you understand the value of your dollar, you need to become conscious about how much you really make. The vast majority of us make a whole lot less than we think we do. We spout our annual salary or sometimes inflate it to friends and the "hot young thang" at the bar we're trying to impress. This, compounded by the perception of what we think we should make or what we think others think we should make, perverts the ability to judge our true income. This often leads to spending as if we make more than we really do.

A mistake that we both made (and know many others who have done the same) was spending our entire first paycheck from our first "real" job. For some reason, when we received our check that payday, we forgot about all of our bills. We went out for dinners and drinks, bought new CDs and clothes, maybe fixed up our apartments a little, but then the electric bill and the gas bill came, then the cable bill, and for some reason, we were short on cash.

There's something humbling about knowing your real income. Earning more or being wealthy doesn't make you any better or worse than anyone else. We will stop there because diving deeper into this topic would be another book. Just understand that your net worth does not determine your value, but understanding your true income is valuable.

In our previous discussion, Understanding the Value of My Dollar, we touched on the idea of how much you make and dismissed the discussion on taxes, but your hourly wage minus taxes is still nothing close to how much you bring home. Grab a recent pay stub. This is the best way to understand how much money you bring home. This will teach you how much money you can truly spend. This exercise will also help you differentiate between your *discretionary* versus *non-discretionary* spending.

A caveat here: those of you who are service providers may make a large portion of your income through tips, commissions, or bonuses. If this is the case, then you should gather a year's worth of pay stubs or pull out your previous year's tax return or W-2.

Below is an example of a typical pay stub. It's broken down into five main sections: earnings, taxes, pre-tax deductions, after -tax deductions, and net pay distributions. We will discuss each section in detail.

Paycheck Summary					
	Gross Earnings	Fed Taxable Gross	Total Taxes	Total Deductions	Net Pay
Current	1,304.13	1,277.18	307.24	26.95	969.94

Earnings				Taxes	
Description	Hours	Rate	Amount	Description	Amount
Regular			1,125.00	Fed Withholdng	157.53
OT 1.5	9.00	19.471154	175.24	Fed MED/EE	18.52
EELif Cred			3.89	Fed OASDI/EE	79.19
				CO Withholdng	52.00
Total:			1,304.13	Total:	307.24

Before-Tax Deductions		After Tax Deductions		Employer Paid Benefits	
Description	Amount	Description	Amount	Description	Amount
Medical	17.50				
Dental	4.00				
Basic Life	0.72				
Disability	4.73			* Taxable	
Total:	26.95	Total:		Total:	

The first section, Earnings, makes sense and is often the figure quoted when discussing how much money you make. Here you have items such as regular pay, overtime pay (if you are a non-exempt employee), and bonuses, if you're so lucky. The annual total here is what will end up on your W-2 at the end of the year. This is your gross salary, but it's by no means how much money you take home.

The second section lists taxes. In most cases, this is the biggest deduction from your earnings. In 2007, the last year for which data is available, it was about 20% of the income for the average worker. Here you should see items such as Federal Withholdings deducted based on how you filled out your W-4. Next, Federal Medicare is taken out at a rate of 1.45% and matched by your employer.

Then Federal OASDI (Old Age Security Disability Insurance) or FICA, which is your payment towards social security; it's 6.2% of your pay (since 1990) and is matched by your employer. You may also have state and local taxes such as municipal or city taxes deducted based on where you work. These are often referred to as "head taxes." Depending on how much you make, you could see this combined total take a chunk of ten to fifty percent of your earnings. This is only the beginning.

The third section is for pre-tax deductions. This is a good section because it directly benefits you. This section helps reduce how much money you pay Uncle Sam in taxes. Here you have categories such as Medical, Dental, Life Insurance, Disability Insurance, flexible benefits like Health Savings Accounts, Child Care, and Medical Gap Insurance and a whole host of 401(k), 403(b), pension and other retirement options. Uncle Sam does not tax you on these items. It's beneficial to increase contributions to your saving and retirement options when possible.

Next, we have after-tax deductions, which include deductions for Employee Stock Purchase Programs and other employee sponsored programs, such as local transportation, assistance, entertainment discounts and employee-responsibility items such as parking fees.

The last section is your Net Pay. This is not the exact amount, but it is the best indicator of your true, take-home income. This is how much money ends up in your pocket or bank account. This is the BIG NUMBER, the one to use when planning your budget and spending.

Notice the difference between your starting number, Earnings (gross pay), and the ending number, Net Pay? In the example, you see Net Pay that is 25.6% lower than the gross pay. How much is it in your case? Being conscious of this number is eye-opening. It's imperative to being Money Conscious. It's possibly the single biggest number in helping you become debt free. It will be the foundation of your financial plan.

This is such a key number, we ask you to pause and calculate your net pay. If you need to annualize your pay because you earn tips and/or bonuses, get 12 months' worth of pay stubs or your previous years' W-2 and do an average. Once you've figured this out, take it to the budget worksheet in the back of this book.

Knowing Where Your Money Goes

Now you have an understanding of the value of a dollar and how many dollars you earn. This puts you head and shoulders above most people when it comes to being Money Conscious and understanding your financial situation. However, this is only the foundation.

We're going to take a moment to underscore the importance in doing the exercises we suggest in this book. It's imperative that you take the time to calculate How Much Money I Make. It's also essential that you follow the next two steps in finding out "Where My Money Goes." These steps will help build a financial plan, which you will do later in the book. Remember that contract you signed? Remember the commitment to pay off your debt that you made to yourself - and hopefully to others? Follow through with these exercises, so you can achieve the goal of living a debt free life.

The next step in understanding your current situation and, eventually, understanding what you need to do to improve your situation, is to understand where your money goes. Where, exactly, does all your money go, and why does it feel like there's never enough? These are common questions for many Americans, including yours truly. These are the two questions we asked that started our journey in becoming debt free.

We started with the following exercise, and what we learned shocked us! We mean - really floored us. We realized something was seriously wrong with our spending habits, and we saw that we could become debt free if we redirected where we were putting our money.

First, break your spending into two categories: essentials or necessities and non-essentials or discretionary. Necessities are things you need to survive - and no, Starbucks is not included in this category. Non-essentials or discretionary spending include things you don't need to survive, but make life a whole lot better.

There will be expenses that appear in both categories. Remember our example of the "Oprah Popcorn"? Popcorn is food and food is a necessity. True, true, but do you need *designer* popcorn for survival?

Your list of necessities should include things such as mortgage or rent, utilities (electricity, gas, water, sewage, and garbage removal), car payments, car insurance, groceries, day care, clothing, medical expenses, phone, student loans - and yes, credit card payments. You'll include credit card payments and other debt payments in the necessities category because this is essential to pay them off.

Next is your list of discretionary spending; entertainment, music, technology, furniture, decorations, gifts, alcohol, dining out, most personal items such as styling aids, snacks and beverages, attending sporting events and concerts, travel, cable TV, the internet, parties, and - for most girls (and even some of the boys), designer anything. This list is massive and could go on for pages, but we think you get the picture.

The next exercise is your second information gathering assignment. In the back of this book is a worksheet, My Spending Analysis, which helps break your spending into these two categories. It will take an hour or two to complete this. Gather all of your credit card statements, checking accounts, savings accounts and any other tools you use to make purchases. Try gathering a whole year's worth, but at a minimum gather the last three months. Remember, you may be able to download them online. Go through each statement and categorize each purchase adding it to the My Spending Analysis worksheet.

In our opinion, this is some of the best time you will spend all year. David took two hours to do all of his credit cards, debit cards, and other payments over a twelve-month period, and it provided him with a vivid picture of his out-of-control spending habits.

Go ahead.

Okay, welcome back! How was it? Are you surprised? Did you find something you didn't like? You likely did. You're probably surprised with some of your spending. This exercise is always an eye-opener. Here are a few surprising discoveries about our particular situation:

1. Over 3 months, David withdrew nearly $1,600 from the ATM that couldn't be accounted for.
2. We were spending between $400-500 a month on groceries for two people in addition to spending hundreds more dining out (what were we eating?).
3. We found we often shopped weekly for groceries but made additional trips throughout the week for other items, such as snacks, desserts, and other non-essentials – to satiate a craving.
4. We were both adding a lot to our credit cards, but were paying very little of the balance each month, which means we were spending more than we were making.
5. There was a disparity between what we were spending on essentials and what we were spending on the non-essentials, especially when it came to clothing, dining out, and entertainment.

6. David noticed that he was nickel-and-diming his credit cards with small purchases, basically creating an illusion that he was not spending that much, but when it all added up at the end of the month, it totaled hundreds (and sometimes thousands) of dollars.
7. We noticed that there were times when we would put purchases on our credit cards even though we had cash in our accounts. This increases the cost of something if the card isn't paid off monthly and tricks us into thinking that we still have cash to spend.
8. We discovered hundreds of dollars a month were being spent on finance charges to credit cards, along with late fees and maximum balance fees.

You know that your habits are similar to ours. Isn't that the reason you bought this book in the first place? You have debt, most of it from unconscious spending and unconscious money management, just as we did. Be honest with yourself and make a true assessment of where your money is going. Are you spending money in at least one category frivolously? Are you a Starbucks-aholic? Do you buy more than the one sale item you swore would be all you would get? Are you nickel and diming yourself?

How many "little items" do you spend your money on each week? Ours was dining out and happy hours. By the way, we aren't alcoholics, but looking at our old spending habits, you might get the impression that we are.

We were spending anywhere between $200 to $300, each of us per weekend, going out to eat with friends and hitting the bars. That was only a couple of martinis and a bottle of wine with dinner. But they were $10 martinis and $60 bottles of wine. That totaled a thousand dollars a month. Funny how happy hour is much longer than an hour, huh? It's the bar that ends up happy.

Compare how much you're spending to how much money you're investing or saving for retirement. How does that make you feel? If you don't change your habits, will you be prepared to retire when you're 55? How about 65? How about 75? If you're curious about how much money you may have based on your current savings, go to www.moneychip.com and use their retirement calculator. You may be as surprised as we were. Hmmm, you may want to rethink how your habits are affecting your future. We are where we are today because of the decisions that we made yesterday. Likewise, we will be where we are tomorrow because of the decisions we make today. Making better decisions today will lead to a better tomorrow!

If considering your current spending habits and your retirement doesn't make you feel good, try this. How does your current spending compare to how much you earn? Hmmm, that didn't make you feel much better, huh? That sucks and we know because we were there. If your spending exceeds your income, and for many Americans (including our government) it does, then you are headed into financial ruin and you must make a course correction. You are living on credit, whether credit cards, home equity loans, or family and friends and that will hold you down for the rest of your life, unless you stop and pay it all off. Remember, not everyone gets a $700,000,000,000 bailout!

This may have been a tedious and painful exercise, but if being Money Conscious is the first principle in living a debt free life, then you must know where your money is going. If you don't know where your money is going, then how can you manage it? The first step in any journey is the furthest away from your goal. Now that you know this, take the next step to a better future: planning how you spend your money.

Believing That a Budget Is a Way of Life

Congratulations! We were afraid that after reading the title of this section, you wouldn't continue reading, and you did! YEA! Either you're a sadist or you trust us. We're not sure what either says about you.

Let's all read the title of this section out loud, "A Budget is a way of life." Good! That wasn't so hard, was it? Again, "A Budget is a way of life." Nice!

This is the least favorite paradigm of the Money Conscious Principle for most people, but therein lies a key reason why so many struggle to live debt free. It's nearly impossible to achieve anything financially without a financial *plan*. That would be like driving to an unfamiliar destination without GPS or directions. Not having a budget or not understanding your cash flow (money in/money out) can put even the richest person into financial trouble. (Google MC Hammer for a real-life example.) You inevitably spend more than you make if you don't have a clear plan for spending and investing.

For starters, B-U-D-G-E-T is *NOT* a four letter word. Really, it's not. It's six. Get those preconceived connotations out of your head. Don't think about a budget as something telling you what you *cannot* do. Consider it as a guide to knowing what you *can* do and when you can do it. We think of it as our roadmap, our GPS to financial freedom. A budget puts down in writing where your money is coming from and where it is going. It gives you the tools to understand when you can buy a new pair of shoes or golf clubs or, more importantly, how much you can invest for your retirement. This is preferable to finding out after the fact that you really couldn't afford that vacation you just took to Mexico, which is the strategy most Americans use.

Understand that we approach a budget a bit differently than most financial experts. We don't consider a budget to be static, but dynamic. Sure, you have regular expenses, typically monthly, which occur. You're also aware of how much you really earn. However, there are times when you have more or less coming and going, especially if the bulk of your pay is from tips, commissions, or bonuses. An additional benefit with a dynamic budget is the ability to adjust your spending when you have the opportunity. For example, paying off bills more quickly, setting more aside for retirement, or saving for that vacation you have in mind. If your life isn't the same day after day, week after week, and month after month, how can your budget be?

We recommend breaking your budget down into monthly segments. This will likely cover all of your bills, since most are due monthly. Use your net pay as your starting figure. This is the "Take home pay" total on the "How Much Money I Make" worksheet that we get to later in this section. First though, let's dissect the budget below.

1st Monthly Pay Check	$1,001.52	2nd Monthly Pay Check	$1,001.52
Roth IRA	($167.00)	Roth IRA	($167.00)
Rent	($450.00)	Car Payment	($292.81)
Insurance	($116.18)	Health Club	($16.58)
Cell Phone	($45.24)	Student Loans	($98.25)
Groceries	($100.00)	Groceries	($100.00)
Gas	($40.00)	Gas	($40.00)
Brokerage	($50.00)	Brokerage	($50.00)
Miscellaneous		Miscellaneous	
Total	$33.10	Total	$236.88

In the example above of John's budget, he's paid twice a month. Some people are paid monthly, bi-weekly, weekly and some on a contract basis, which could be any pay cycle. Use the timing that makes the most sense for you. The objective with building a budget is to work your spending around your pay cycle. The reason is, if you don't plan appropriately, you'll spend all of your pay before covering your necessities.

In this example, notice how John paid his cell phone bill, rent and gas with his first paycheck of the month. When he received his second paycheck of the month, he paid his car loan, gym membership, and student loans. In both instances, he immediately deducted what he owed to cover his bills, which allowed him to make sure he had the money to pay them on time and contribute to his retirement and taxable savings accounts. What's left was a balance to use as discretionary spending for the rest of the pay period.

Notice that there's a considerable difference in available discretionary spending after all bills are paid and contributions to savings are made the first half of the month compared to the second half of the month. To balance this out, John would set aside $101.80 from his second paycheck to use with the following months first paycheck. This way he always had $134.99 to spend each pay period. Some of these expenses, such as groceries and rent, were so low because they were shared with David.

Larger expenses, such as mortgage and rent, may be difficult for some to pay and have enough left over to cover other expenses within the same pay period. In such cases, we suggest dividing larger bills by the number of paychecks you receive each month. You may either pay this divided portion directly to the company to whom you owe the money or set it aside until the bill comes due. We prefer the former.

Your non-discretionary fixed expenses are the items that you deduct first. These are items that rarely change in their amount due, such as rent/mortgage, car payment, insurance, day care, credit card payments (we'll discuss this in detail later), student loans, cable TV, and so on.

Your bills that fluctuate, such as groceries, gas, electricity, phone, etc. are deducted second. You can refer to the Where My Money Goes worksheet below to find a listing of some suggestions and space to add some of your own. Reviewing the history of these expenses will allow you to estimate what you should expect.

Knowing Where
My Money Goes Worksheet

Expense	Dollar Amount	Percentage
Rent/Mortgage		
Insurance		
Car Payment		
Gas		
Utilities		
Credit Card Payments		
Groceries		
Clothing		
Entertainment		
Medical		
Home		
Dining Out		

At the bottom of all of these deductions, both fixed and fluctuating, is your total. Hopefully this number is positive. If so, congratulations! You have disposable income to work with. For some, this may not be a positive number. We'll help address that.

Below we list expenses under categories of Discretionary Fixed, Discretionary Fluctuating, Non-Discretionary Fluctuating and Non-Discretionary Fixed.

Non-Discretionary Fixed	Non-Discretionary Fluctuating
• Rent/Mortgage • Car payment • Insurance • HOA payments • Student loan payments • Credit card payments • Investments	• Gas/Electric/Water • Groceries • Gas • Auto maintenance • Business clothes • Dry cleaning
Discretionary Fixed	**Discretionary Fluctuating**
• Cable • Cell phone, not including data and text • Gym membership • Internet • Kids' activities	• Movies • Books/Magazine subscriptions • Dining out/Drinks/Going Out • Clothing (non-work required) • Home decorating • Coffee shops • Birthday/Holiday/Wedding Gifts

Looking at these expenses, it's easy to see how easy it is to overspend. Did you buy too much of a house or car? Do you overspend on groceries? (Think gourmet items.) Are the kids in too many after-school activities? How often are you out to eat or to the movies?

To remedy this, you will need to consider cutting back on discretionary expenses, finding a way to increase income, or finding a more practical way of meeting your necessities. Can you move into a cheaper home or switch to a less expensive car – in other words, cut back on the fixed expenses? In the next section, Living Below Your Means, we'll discuss ways to do this.

It's all about money in and money out; making sure you have less going out than coming in. Ponder this. We'll revisit when we discuss the fourth principle.

At this point, we want to congratulate you. Go ahead - stand up and pat yourself on the back – you deserve it! Having gone through the exercises of Knowing How Much I Make, Where My Money Goes and then understanding that A Budget is a Way of Life, you're becoming Money Conscious. Even if these are the only tools you take away from this book, your financial life will improve. Over time, you'll start looking at money and spending differently and reap the financial rewards of being Money Conscious. If you continue, you will see the other principles build on top of what you've learned.

Now, let's add a bit of Gingko Biloba to your Money Consciousness. Let's discuss a few tools to heighten your awareness of your financial circumstances.

Additional Windows into Money Consciousness

What do we mean by Money Conscious - Gingko Biloba? These are the tools that will ignite your Money Consciousness. These tools will make being Money Conscious easier and, if used properly, catapult you to the financial success that you envision for yourself.

Consider using three different accounts to manage your money. The first holds your monthly, non-discretionary funds (our Bill Pay account). The second holds your discretionary funds and the third holds your emergency savings. The purpose of keeping separate accounts is two-fold. This method will allow you to both obtain a quick and accurate snapshot of where your finances are at any point in time. It will, also, prevent you from commingling your funds, decreasing the risk of dipping into the funds of an account intended for another purpose.

The key to managing these separate accounts under normal circumstances is to have your paychecks directly deposited into each according to your monthly needs. A pre-determined, specified amount is direct-deposited into your non-discretionary account, the residual is direct-deposited into your discretionary account, and any necessary transfers are made from your discretionary account into your emergency savings account to maintain your three-to-six months' worth of expenses.

We feel that the older one gets, the higher the potential risk for needing to tap into emergency savings. For this reason, an older person should keep closer to six months' worth of expenses in their emergency savings account, while a younger person can get away with as little as three months' worth. In both cases, these funds should be invested conservatively in products such as money market funds or short term CDs, with no more than a three-month maturity.

The emergency savings account, like your non-discretionary account, should not have ATM access, a debit card, credit card, checking, or the ability to easily transfer to a linked account. Refraining from adding these account features will limit your access and, therefore, decrease the chances of dipping into them for reasons that are not legitimate emergencies. The benefit of being Money Conscious and having an emergency savings account is that it acts as your Xanax, or chill pill. When an emergency arises, such as a car breaking down, loss of a job, unexpected medical issues, it allows you to take a step back from the situation and consider where and how you should pay for it. You can ask yourself the questions; am I able to cut back on discretionary spending - or possibly my non-discretionary spending - to cover the unexpected expense, or should I dip into the emergency savings account under the condition that I will pay it back immediately? This is a safety net that provides immense personal security.

When opening an account, you should find one that is yielding the most interest as possible. Not easy these days, but first consider local banks and credit unions, as they often provide higher rates because of lower marketing and overheard costs. Also consider larger banks, as well as brokerage firms, because they have a little more leverage that allow them to be more competitive. Find a bank account or money market account with high-yielding interest, so that you earn the most while your cash is sitting in limbo.

Account Breakdown

- Non-discretionary Account

    o Funds are direct-deposited into this account on a per paycheck basis to cover bills, both fixed and fluctuating.
    o Ideally, always have a months' worth of expenses sitting here to provide a cushion.
    o Bills are set up to be paid either through bill-pay or automatic withdrawal, so all bills are paid in full and on time every month.
    o No ATM, debit or credit card on this account, just checks to cover groceries and the occasional bill that needs to be sent via snail mail.

- Emergency Savings

    o The funds in this account cover three to six times monthly expenses and are to be accessed for true emergencies only.

o No ATM, debit, credit card or checks on this account; only option to withdrawal funds from this account is to drive to the bank, credit union, or brokerage and ask for your money.

o These funds are invested in safe, secure, and liquid holdings, such as short term CDs.

- Discretionary Account

o This money is play money to use entirely as you wish.

o If you find a surplus in this account (more than you *honestly* need to play with), use it to pay off debt, invest it or set it aside for a more expensive treat, like a vacation.

Let's apply a real life scenario to this. You establish your accounts as outlined above and it's the end of a very cold February. March comes and you get your friendly bill in the mail or email. Once opened, you notice that, because it was so cold the previous month, the bill is $60 higher than usual.

You hop onto your computer to access your three accounts and to see if you have the money available to cover this unexpected increase. You first look in your non-discretionary account. If you have the funds here, great! If you don't, you check your discretionary account to see if you either have the extra $60 already available or if you can tighten your spending for the month of March to make up the extra cost. If neither of these are options, then you can fall back onto your emergency savings. This is why it's there.

When your next paycheck is direct-deposited into your accounts, you take $60 from your discretionary account and transfer it to your emergency savings, so you continue to maintain your required minimum emergency savings balance.

Another tool for the Money Conscious is setting up automatic payments. Bill Pay and automatic drafts from your bank accounts are life savers. How many times have you forgotten to pay a bill or paid it late and then had to pay a late fee? Auto deductions and Bill Pay can take care of all this for you. Once you establish these automatic payments, the rest is on auto-pilot. Your bills will either be drafted from your account or a check is automatically generated to cover your bills each month. This is one way we can all live like a celebrity. Do you think the Kardashians worry about their mortgage being paid every month? Heck no! They have an accountant take care of this for them – although, we seriously doubt they would worry about it, even if they didn't have an accountant.

Here's how to set this up. Your mortgage is due on the 5th of each month. Consequently, you set up an automatic deduction out of your non-discretionary account on the 2nd of every month. Then your insurance is due on the 15th of each month and you set up an automatic deduction on the 12th. Once you establish this, everything has been taken care of for you. Your only responsibility is to review your monthly statements, making sure your payments are timely and that the amount due each month has not changed.

Another benefit with this tool is that often companies will give you a discount if you let them make automatic deductions from your account to cover bills. Our mortgage lender gives us a 1/8 percentage point discount to allow them to automatically deduct our monthly mortgage payment from our account. That is not much of a savings on a monthly basis, but over the life of a 30-year loan, it adds up. On our $130,000 loan, it's a savings of $3,283.20. That is more money for us.

Making your budget automatic is a huge step in being Money Conscious. It may sound contradictory, but it's not. By eliminating as much of the minutia with paying bills and investing money as possible, it frees you to perform the high-level management of your finances.

Another technique in being Money Conscious is to shift your payments in line with your pay cycle. You can do this by contacting companies you make payments to and ask them to adjust your payable dates. This helps you ensure that all of your bills will be paid on time and in full. By explaining to these companies that you're creating a budget, they will likely work with you. Some may not be able to, but most will, and it can't hurt to ask.

It's time for an analogy. Consider your body. You must breathe, right? It's a necessity. How conscious are you about your every breath? How conscious would you be about your surroundings if you had to focus on every breath? Most likely your surroundings would fall in the level of importance. But because breathing for most of us is effortless, we can direct our attention to other things. The same is true with your money. If you automate as much as possible, then you can focus on the other things. Expand your Money Consciousness.

We have one more, excellent financial tool. This is your financial report card. We know it doesn't sound exciting. But remember when you worked extra hard and you got that "A" in school? This is exactly what will happen to your FICO score if you follow the 4: The Four Principles of Living a Debt Free Life. *(Sorry to those of you who never got that "A"!)*

FICO? FIC-U!! No, don't be offended. We're not swearing at you. Why are we going to teach you about something as potentially offensive as a FICO? Well, because it could save you tens, if not thousands of dollars over the course of your life. That's money with which you can pay down your debt more quickly or put towards more important things like retirement, education, or your home. By the end of this section, you will be telling everyone to FICO.

FICO (Fair Isaac Corporation) is a credit score. Whenever you look to a lender such as a bank or credit union for a loan, either for your mortgage or a car loan, they use your FICO score to determine how much of a credit risk you are. The less risky you are as a debt holder, the better your FICO score, and the better your interest rates will be on your loans.

FICO.org defines a credit score as "an estimate of your credit risk based on a snapshot of your credit report at a particular point in time".[4] We'll elaborate in more detail later in the book. For the time being, we have some phone numbers below for you to call to request your personal credit history. These will take time to get to you. Call now, so you have them when need them for a future exercise.

Another way of increasing your Money Consciousness is to understand how financial institutions view you and how you compare to other Americans. Because of this, we suggest contacting all three credit agencies (Equifax, TransUnion and Experian) and ask them for your credit report. For Equifax, either go to www.equifax.com or call 800-685-1111. For TransUnion, either go to www.transunion.com or call 877-322-8228. For Experian, either go to www.experian.com or call 888-397-3742.

Or, you can go to www.annualcreditreport.com and request a report from all three agencies at once (this company doesn't have a direct phone number). Under the Fair Credit Reporting Act, all Americans are entitled to one free, personal credit report from each credit rating agency per year. It will take about a month for these to arrive in your mailbox, so order them now so you can get them as soon as possible for a future exercise.

Knowing How Much Money I Make Worksheet

Earnings
Regular Pay
OT
Bonus
                    Earnings Total $ -
Before Tax Deductions
Medical
Dental
Basic Life Ins.
Disability Ins.
401k/403b/457 Contribution
FSA Health (Flex Benefit Plan)
    Before Tax Deductions Total $ -
Taxes
Federal Taxes
Fed. Medicare
Fed. OASDI
State Withholding
County Withholding
City Withholding
                    Taxes Total $ -
After Tax Deductions
Charitable Contributions
Roth/IRA Contributions
Employee Stock Purchase Plan
Child Support/Alamony
Wage Garnishment
    After Tax Deductions Total $ -

**Take Home Pay (What I
really make)** $ -

Summary of Money Consciousness

- The value of your dollar is determined by how much money you make and how much money you have.
- You need to review your pay stubs to determine how much you really bring home in pay.
- Reviewing your expenses for a year is an eye opener to where your money is going and lays the foundation to help you figure out where you can save.
- Dynamic budgets are your friends.
- Through a little creativity and awareness, you can take your Money Consciousness to the next level: direct deposits, automatic withdrawals or Bill Pay, non-discretionary and discretionary accounts, emergency savings, and FICO.

Chapter Six:

Principle Two:
Live Below Your Means

Introduction to the Living Below Your Means Principle

At the heart of living a debt free life is the principle of Living Below Your Means. We know we sound like your lecturing parents. Though there was truth in their advice, it's possible to still have a fun and rewarding life while living below your means. We'll elaborate on how to have fun while being money conscious later. For now, let's focus on the habits that help you control your spending.

As we've discussed so far, most of us can expect to bring home a certain amount of money on a regular basis. If you don't have a job, this principle still applies just as much as if you do. We both began to understand many of these habits when David was laid off and living on his severance pay.

If you get a chance to talk with someone who lived during The Great Depression (1929 - 1939), you'll learn about how difficult it was. They'll tell you what it was like not knowing where their next meal was coming from. They'll describe what the scarcity of food was like or how their fathers felt about not having a steady job.

David's father used to tell him the story of how his grandfather would come home after working all night long, tired and ready for bed. Before he would go to bed himself, he would wake up his children to ask them if they were hungry. This was his way of making sure that his children didn't suffer the way he did when he was younger. The Great Depression was not great - it was truly depressing.

In most cases, these Depression Era survivors will give useful advice. They'll tell you to appreciate what you have because they had nothing. They'll tell you to save what can be used again, like plastic bags, aluminum foil, old clothes, even buttons from those old clothes. Another piece of wisdom that they'll share is the principle of Living Below Your Means. In other words, don't spend more than you have.

Today it's not so easy to Live Below Your Means. There are so many demands for your money: mortgages, groceries and gas, cars, sports for the kids, phone, Internet, and a myriad of other demands. The fundamentals for Living Below Your Means focus on *contentment* or, another way of saying it - enjoying life with what you already have.

Whether or not you choose to be happy with what you have is up to you. We touch on this in other areas throughout this book, but it bears repeating because it's important and is why we dedicate a whole section to this principle. We are both believers in the Law of Abundance, in that there is plenty to go around for everyone. But we also believe that everyone doesn't always get an equal share. Some people are born into the right situation, some are presented with more advantageous opportunities and others work really hard and, consequently, have more. When someone has more than we do, we understand that it doesn't mean we are worth *less*. They just have more. They could also have a lot more other things - such as stress, medical issues, family problems, etc.

How do we feel when someone has more than we do? We focus on not being jealous of what they have. That jealousy can cause us to go out and rack up debt on our credit cards. Instead, we concentrate on being thankful for what we have, understanding that we can work for more. Satisfaction with what you have and the fact that what you have is *good enough* is a key characteristic to helping you get out and stay out of debt.

The Psychology of Living Below Your Means

What allows you to live above your means when you rationally understand that you cannot? What void is there in your life that causes you to continually spend more than you make?

Here are a few fundamental ideals that are included in the principle of Living Below Your Means: separate needs from wants, don't blow the bank on a good time, learn contentment, avoid living up to others' expectations, differentiate wise purchases from instant gratification, don't succumb to status symbol purchases, and understand the difference between long-term planning and the short-term effect of your purchases. We're going to take each of these values and break them down.

Distinguishing Needs from Wants

What is the difference between a need and a want? According to Webster's, a need is a physical or mental requirement for your well-being. In other words, without it you won't be well and will likely not survive. To want, on the other hand, is to have a strong desire for something, whether necessary or unnecessary for your survival. Let's look at an example.

Do you need a million dollars? Okay, bad example. If you had a million dollars, then you wouldn't need to finish this book. Do you need a place to live? Yes. What kind of place do you need in order to survive? How about the 40,000 square foot penthouse condo that Candy Spelling bought for a cool $42 million? For most of us, it's easy to see that this particular place would be a want rather than a need. Personally, we live in a 1,008 square-foot condo and don't understand the need for 40,000 square feet.

Let's look at another example. In the span of about 15 years, the cell phone has gone from a luxury to a necessity. We aren't going to debate the value of cell phones. People all across the world are more productive and connected because of them. But let's talk about needs versus wants with regards to a cell phone and the iPhone.

We both love Apple and Apple products and, in fact, are shareholders.* Their products are great looking, easy to use, reliable, and fun. With the release of each new iPhone, millions of people clamor to buy one. In fact the release of the iPhone 5S and 5C in September 2013 sold 9 million phones worldwide in the first three days. That's right, 9 million. As with the first iPhone even today people are willing to wait in line overnight to increase their chances of being one of the first to have the latest version. First-adopters are willing to pay anywhere from $200 to $900 to buy the phone plus upwards of $130 a month for a contract with one of the major carriers. What's the difference between a standard cell phone and the iPhone? One word: coolness. That's it. The iPhone is cool. It has a touch screen, a built in iPod and now even a fingerprint reader, along with a handful of useful and fun apps.

But, what is its primary purpose? It's a telephone. First-generation buyers spent $1,800 in that first year for a telephone when they could've gotten a free, basic cell phone from AT&T with a plan for unlimited talk and text for about $60 a month. That's $720 per year. That's still a fair chunk of change, but it's a savings of over $1,000 the first year and about $500 per year after compared to the iPhone. Need versus want?

With your spending, you must view the whole picture. If you spend your money on one thing, that means you have less to spend on another. The $1,800 spent in that first year to have the first iPhone didn't go towards savings or making a down payment on a house or a car. It didn't go towards mortgage payments or a charity. It went to Apple and AT&T.

The best way to determine if something is a need or a want is to ask yourself two questions. First, "Would you make this purchase with the last penny you had?" The second is, "Do you need to make this purchase right now?" In other words, can you make do without it for a while? Applying these two questions to all of your purchases will help you Live Below Your Means.

A great example of how we have applied these questions to our personal lives has to do with our laptop computers. Both of our laptops are over five years old, but act like they're ten. In the world of computers, that's ancient! We've had to take both of our computers in for repairs on several occasions and had to replace the hard drive on one. Of course, being the young and trendy people we like to think we are, we would love to buy new laptops, preferably Apple's Mac Book Air. But because we are Money Conscious and understand the value of Living Below Your Means, we've held off on these purchases. In fact, we've held off long enough to use our current computers to write this whole book. Eventually we will take the plunge, but for now, we will make do while we save up for our new laptops.

* This is not a recommendation. Please contact a financial advisor to determine what investments are appropriate for you.

Differentiating Wise Purchases from Impulse Purchases

Have you ever walked into the grocery store to buy one thing and walked out with three, four, five - or even ten items that you had no intention of buying?

We often go in for some bread and come out with cheese, olives, crackers, cookies, and a pint of ice cream. Three dollars just turned into twenty-five! How does this happen?

Ever wonder why the checkout counter at the store places the candy down low and magazines up high on the "Last-Ditch-Effort-To-Sell-Something-To-You" rack? Well, who is generally around three feet high? Kids. How many people do you see staring at the tabloids long enough until they eventually throw one in their cart because they desperately need to find out what's up with Nicki Minaj and Mariah Carey or find out if Lindsay's finally going to jail? What do all these purchases have in common? They're impulse buys. In all fairness, we're guilty of this, too. No one gets a "Get out of Jail Free Card" on this one. The reality is that we add so many extra items to our shopping carts, or we all too frequently run to the store to buy the latest gadget we just saw on TV, all because of a sudden desire - an impulse.

How do you keep up your guard when you're shopping? The key is preparation. We only go shopping when we know what we need, where we need to get it, and approximately how much it will cost. This helps keep our shopping within our budget.

Purchases, like life partners, should be made with a clear, level head and with intent. The bigger the purchase, the more valuable this advice. Bigger purchases, such as cars, homes, appliances, or Twitter followers (kidding!) should be made only after doing some research. You want to find the best product or service for the price that you can afford.

You don't always want to sacrifice quality to save a few bucks, since it may cost you more in the long run. This is why taking your time and thinking costly purchases through is being Money Conscious. Though the consequences for smaller purchases aren't as grave, the practice is still prudent because often it is the smaller purchases that are easily dismissed - but quickly add up. We will discuss all this in more detail in How to Go Shopping.

Not Blowing Up Your Bank Account for a Good Time

We love to have a good time with our friends and family . . . and, let's face it – a little wine or beer (or a Rita or two). More often than not, having fun leads to spending money . . . very often because of the wine, beer, or Ritas! Sadly a paradigm that has poisoned our American brains is "more is better." This is obvious when it comes to our spending habits. We have conditioned ourselves into believing that the more expensive wine is better, the more expensive car is better, the more expensive vacation is better, or the more expensive concert seats or the more expensive golf clubs are better.

This is where quality versus quantity comes into play. Sometimes a movie at home with a pizza and a few beers is all we need to relax and have a good time. This NSE ("not so expensive") entertainment can cost a group of four to six people less than $100. If that same group of people went out for dinner, they'd easily spend twice that amount and possibly three or four. The problem is that most of the time we don't do just pizza and beer. Usually it's the trendy new restaurant - and then the hip bar downtown.

NSE stands for "**N**ot **S**o **E**xpensive". We aren't suggesting that we give up on quality. Rather, we suggest finding things of good quality that are more in line with your budget. This is our E.V.O.O. (Extra Virgin Olive Oil). Take that, Rachel Ray!

Case in point: we were in San Francisco one weekend and went out with a group of friends for dinner and drinks one evening. The next morning, or afternoon actually, we woke up slightly hung over - and poorer by $500 per couple. You read that right. Five couples spent a total of $2,500 in one night. What makes this story more painful is we all agreed that neither the food nor the drinks were that great. Did we need to do this? No. We could've found a less expensive restaurant to dine at and cut back on our number of cocktails while still having a good time. Situations like this are when it benefits us to take cash - Cash Being King, of course.

This is a perfect segue into our discussion of how money does not equate to happiness. Sociological research and our own simple observations show that one's income and wealth play a small role in one's happiness.[5] There are many other factors that are integral to our happiness. Consider, for a moment, celebrities. How many train wrecks do we have to see until we understand that money and/or fame does not make one happy? Why couldn't Whitney Houston figure out how to be happy? Why was Elvis Presley hooked on drugs? Why, after winning a small fortune, couldn't Anna Nicole Smith get her life in order? Why was Leona Helmsley such a B*/@h? Estimations put her net worth as high as $5 billion and yet she has gone down in history as "The Queen of Mean," having left her entire fortune to her dog.

Boston.com, a local news organization in Massachusetts, quoted Bob Kenny, executive director of More Than Money, a nonprofit group in Concord, MA that studies the effect money has on people's lives as saying, "It is the great American myth. Everybody thinks the more money they have, the happier they'll be; that everything would be better 'if I just hit the lottery.' It just is not true."[6]

Marilyn Elias of *USA Today* began her 2002 article "Psychologists Now Know What Makes People Happy" by saying, "The happiest people surround themselves with family and friends, *do not care about keeping up with The Jones' next door* (emphasis ours), lose themselves in daily activities and, most important, forgive easily."[7] She went on to describe several studies done at the time to support this statement. Notice that wealth, money, income, and any word related to money were not included in her findings.

In later sections, we'll discuss how to vacation, date, and grocery shop on a budget. It may be hard to believe, but it is possible to have a life and not go broke. It just takes creativity and flexibility.

Not Living Up to the Expectations of Others

What of your friends, parents, in-laws, or even spouse? When it comes to the things you have, whose expectations should you be concerned with?

Shouldn't it be your own? It should be, but the fact is that too often we're concerned with what others think. Truth is, this starts early on in our lives and is, to some degree, taught to us by loved ones and by marketers. Ahhh, gotta love those marketers!

Think about the "Back to School" shopping scam. Remember that? Some of us relive it every year with our own children. Why's it so important to have tons of new clothes for the beginning of every school year? Oh, and then again after Christmas break? That's right. Then there's spring break. The reality is we probably got a new pair of jeans back in May, so why aren't they good enough come December? They're denim; they're made to last. Because this is how we show off. Why? Validation. If we're validated, we're cool, and people will like us. Guess what? We still do it today as grownups. Whether it's with clothing or a house or a car or golf clubs or a new purse, we still do it. We're still trying to live up to other's expectations.

How do you manage relationships with friends and not live up to their expectations? For starters, it takes a bit of courage. Tell them you're cutting back and need to stay home this weekend. Ask if they want to join you. In many cases, they will.

You learn so much more about your friends when you do simple things with them. You talk, play games, cook dinner together, and watch movies. What we've found is that many of our friends are in the same boat, and we talk about strategies for getting out of debt. You'll find that your friends who don't have money issues are often in agreement to stay home or to do less expensive things. This could be why they don't have money problems. They're more than happy to stay in and cut back on spending. Everyone has their own financial goals that are more easily achieved with spending less.

Two friends of ours were married a few summers back. The year leading up to their wedding and honeymoon, they spent many weekend nights at our condo eating dinners, drinking wine, and playing games. This let them save cash for their wedding and a beautiful honeymoon to Spain. Since we ended up saving so much money ourselves, we joined them for the last few days of the honeymoon for an amazing time in Ibiza.

Being honest with yourself about what you can and cannot afford and admitting that *things* won't make you happy will go a long way to financial freedom. As they say, "The truth will set you free" or, in this case, "the truth will set you *debt* free." This will reduce stress and increase happiness. The lack of stress and anxiety will take years off your face, which is better than spending thousands on Botox.

Not Making Status Symbol Purchases

Times are tough these days. We understand. We all have a reputation to live up to. You want to look like a professional at the office and come across as though you can compete with the best in your field. You want your children to look presentable when they're with their friends' or at school. You don't want your house to be the one on the block that brings down property values. We get it. It's not easy.

This habit is similar to avoiding living up to others' expectations. How wrong is it if your child went to play with their friends with a hole in their jeans? They're going to get dirty anyway. What if your lawn isn't the greenest on the block? Wouldn't you enjoy a weekend of not manicuring, mowing and fertilizing it, anyway?

Let's take this to the extreme because - hey, why not? Status symbol purchases are those purchases we believe validate us in the eyes of others. These purchases can be almost anything and are hardly necessary. They're the new toy that everyone else has and, therefore, we must. It's a house that costs twice as much as we can afford and three times more than we need. They're designer T-shirts that cost a few hundred dollars to buy because it has some random guy's name on it - and only costs nickels to make.

Before we got together, David would buy all his jeans from the Gap which, at the time, ran about $50 per pair. After we got together, John convinced David to get a few pair of jeans from Abercrombie & Fitch because they were a better brand and looked nicer - and people would notice him. They did and David liked this. Eventually, David's judgment became clouded, and he was talked into buying some jeans from Diesel, starting at about $200 per pair. These looked even better and were "designer." Again, he liked the attention, but this drive for status symbol-quality denim was building up on his credit card and keeping him from achieving his long-term financial goals. Guess where David bought his last pair of jeans? (Hint: not A&F or Diesel.)

How do you live by this mantra of not making status symbol purchases? Again, this requires you to plan ahead, know what you want and when you can honestly afford it, before you make rash purchases. This is where understanding that a Budget is a Way of Life is so important. You need to think about your spending and be honest with the reasons for your purchases.

Short-Term Non-Planning vs. Long-Term Planning

Another focus of Living Below Your Means is factoring in the "opportunity consequences," or the cost of your purchases. Huh? It's the short-term versus long-term impact of your spending. We touched a bit on it during the discussion of the iPhone. Remember that $130 per month contract, the extra $500 to $1000 per year we would be spending for the AT&T service? Let's look at another example of this.

By now we're all too familiar with the housing crisis that started in 2008. What misconception got us into trouble? This includes everyone from Main Street to Wall Street to Pennsylvania Avenue – believing that home prices would never stop appreciating. The truth is that they rarely do, but it does happen. How does long-term versus short-term planning play into this? It's directly connected because we were only focusing on the current and the near-term outlook of the housing market and not considering historical and long-term possibilities, which are directly tied to the type of loans that were created. As a result of our shortsightedness, we misled ourselves (with the help of banks and the government) into having a false sense of what we could afford.

Let's use a slightly above average, middle-American couple bringing home about $100,000 per year as an example. A good rule of thumb is to not spend more than two and a half to three times your annual salary on purchasing a home, assuming you have no other major debts, such as car and student loans or credit cards. That middle-American family shouldn't look at homes costing more than $300,000.

But what happened with the housing boom between 1998 through 2006? We were told by real estate brokers, mortgage brokers, lenders, banks - even the Federal Reserve chairman - that we could afford homes five, six even ten times our annual salary. How? We were buying these houses, historically out of reach, with "designer loans", such as short-term adjustable - rate mortgages or interest-only loans.

This directly links to the false notion that homes would increase in value five or even ten percent every year. When there was enough equity in our home, we would refinance and get a lower payment or sell the house for a profit. But as we now know, prices don't always go up. They drop, too. In some areas they dropped significantly, which left millions with mortgages costing more than the houses were worth. This is called being upside down on your mortgage. To get out of these houses, you would have to pay the bank to take it back or to sell it to someone else at a loss; thus, the flood of foreclosures that took place after 2008.

All America was doing was using the inflated equity in homes to finance a lifestyle that was very short term: vacations, new clothes, new cars, newer and even bigger homes, and sometimes paying down credit cards, only to max them out again. We were enjoying this instant gratification lifestyle at the expense of building sound equity in our homes or actually rolling the equity back into our homes when we refinanced to lower monthly payments – instead of using the added financial freedom to secure our future.

John's purchase of his new Volkswagen Jetta is a prime example of the consequence of short-term planning. He knew he wanted a black Volkswagen Jetta and went to the dealership and bought it without considering whether or not he could afford it. As a result, he leased the new car for five years, than bought it out at the end of the term by financing it for another three years, paying high interest on both the lease and the loan for a total of 8 years.

When considering short-term versus long-term gratification, as it relates to Living Below Your Means, this is a great time to consider the consequences of your purchases. How will it impact your retirement plan? How will this impact your ability to pay for your kid's college tuition? What other sacrifices will not only *you* have to make, but the rest of your family? If you work as hard as you do for your loved ones, then maybe some of those impulse purchases aren't necessary. They say a little sacrifice is good for the soul. It is also good for the wallet.

Learning Contentment

Remember in the beginning of *Harry Potter and the Chamber of Secrets* when it's Harry's stepbrother's birthday, and he goes into a rage because he didn't get as many presents as the prior year? It was a clear example of a greedy and selfish child. In the right circumstances, we're all like him, though. It seems natural to want more. More ice cream, more cake, more presents - more, more, more. We learn about getting more as children, and it sticks with us as adults. It's fun to get more.

One of David's guilty pleasures is popcorn. He has been known to sit down with a bag of microwave popcorn and eat the whole thing by himself. That isn't bad, but then he pops another one in the microwave. Then there's only one bag left in the box. So, out it comes and down it goes. Yes, three bags of popcorn in one sitting! Why? What is it that makes him do this? It's the instant gratification of more. We live in a fast-paced world, and we need everything right now. With all the glitz it's easy to get distracted from the most important thing in life - and that is simply being happy.

This is how we suggest learning contentment: focus on what makes you *truly* happy. Our purpose for writing this book is to take what we learned the hard way and share it with others. Knowing that you could use our mistakes, the solutions we created, and the principles we learned regarding getting and staying out of debt to help others in the same situation excited us. Therefore, as Marilyn Elias alluded to in the *USA Today* article mentioned previously, our suggestion is to find one or two things in your life that really excite you and can increase your personal happiness.

The key here is to focus on the non-material. Some people love the outdoors, so take your family hiking. Others love to read. Volunteer at a local school or after-school program to teach children how to read. For some, it's cooking. Cook an inexpensive, delicious feast for someone you love - or someone you barely know. Find a career doing what you love and in which you find personal satisfaction. Maybe you don't know what you love to do. Now is a great time to figure that out. If your passion is shopping, maybe you need to become a personal shopper and spend other people's money!

A study done by Dr. Caroline West from The University of Sydney suggests that we derive more personal satisfaction from experiences than we do from objects and material things. Consider this as you look for your passion.

We volunteer on occasion at a homeless shelter, making and serving food. This has taught us both some valuable lessons. We also volunteer at a center that delivers meals to the terminally ill. This puts life into perspective. Who cares about the new Prada bag or how our fantasy football team is doing when someone is just trying to make it to their next meal. Volunteering is a valuable and rewarding experience that can help you discover what's important in life. Spending your time focusing on someone else also helps you learn more about yourself.

How to Have a Life

Although contentment and Living Below Your Means makes sense, like the saying goes, "Easier said than done!" This is true unless you learn the skills, plan it out, and put it into practice. Practice is the key here. Like most principles in our lives, once we become aware of them and use them over and over, they become second nature. How do you do that? Next, are several examples of how we learned to live below our means. We hope you will see that it is actually easy to do and can even be fun.

How to Grocery Shop

The average family of four spends about $8,000 per year on groceries. With a pet, they spend hundreds more. That's a lot of money. As we mentioned previously, one of the worst habits is to go into a store without a plan of action. This is never truer than when you go grocery shopping.

For most of us, grocery shopping means meandering up and down aisles, grabbing anything that looks good - some fruit, maybe cereal, milk, pizza, chips, cookies, a few chicken breasts, some vegetables . . . what else looks good? We choose based on impulse with the hope that we can throw together a meal or two when we get home.

Even though we spend more than a week's worth of grocery money on this trip, we'll still need to go back later in the week to get what we missed. An added consequence of this process is that we buy a bunch of snack foods, empty calories that don't make up meals, but help to keep us nice and fat.

Okay then, how should you grocery shop? The answer to that is to shop with *intent*. We suggest going to the grocery store once a week. The less you're there, the less you'll spend. If you only go once a week, then you need to know what will get you through the week. This doesn't mean loading the cart until it overflows so you won't have to go back. The idea is to have a plan, and a plan means a menu, and a menu means a grocery list.

Ugh! What a chore, right?! It isn't that bad. If you use a few tricks, you can create a menu for the week and a shopping list in about 20-30 minutes. How? The basis for your menu and your list are the exact same thing: the weekly sales flyer. Here's how it works.

All grocery stores have weekly sales. They do this to entice you to buy specific products referred to as "loss leaders." It's these products that stores are willing to lose money on. Why? Because they know these will get you into the store and that you'll buy additional items that aren't on sale but are marked up to provide the store enough to cover their loss - and more. They know your weakness and know that hardly anyone goes to the store for one item or buys only what they intend on buying, as we discussed in the section "Differentiate between a Wise Purchase and an Impulse Buy." Ultimately, you end up spending more than you want - and on items not on sale. What to do? Turn the game on them.

We collect the flyers from each store in our area and use only the sale items to create both our grocery list and our weekly menu. The key is to never deviate from the list and stick to your weekly menu. (We'll talk about exceptions later.) Creating a grocery list is important because it makes it easier to get *only* what you intend. A list, also, lets you match coupons to sale items.

We've signed up for our local Sunday paper - and only the Sunday paper - because the rest is a waste of time. Any news you need to get can be found on the Internet for free. The Sunday paper, however, includes coupons. If used wisely, you'll only pay for an annual subscription, but end up saving more than enough to cover the subscription.

Smart phones make coupon hunting easier. Open a Twitter account and follow individuals who direct others to coupons. There are apps you can download to your phone and websites, like coupons.com, that list coupons at your fingertips.

Use only the coupons to buy what you *need* and on items you use already. Don't get sold on new items that you don't need. We've found that since we rarely eat processed foods, which are money-drainers, we mostly clip coupons for products such as shampoo and conditioner, soap and detergent – common household items. Occasionally, there are offers to get an item for free if you buy another. For example, get a carton of free eggs with the purchase of a gallon of milk and a package of butter. These are all items we use and, therefore, we use the coupon and get the items when we need them.

We only take advantage of these coupons if we actually need the item or items for that week. Don't get pressured into buying something simply because you have a coupon or because it's going to expire. Not only will this coupon clipping fulfill the hunter-gatherer in you, it will save you huge sums of money.

This is where it gets fun. We have actually made using coupons and going grocery shopping a game for ourselves. At the bottom of most receipts, grocery stores itemize the dollar amount spent and the percentage saved. We've found that by using coupons on items we already need and that are on sale, we can save 50% or more sometimes. There have been times when some items end up being free. It's become a challenge to get the most off our total bill as possible. Our personal best is 56% and we're not talking about just buying a few items. This was a full grocery cart that started well above $100 and ended up costing less than $50! In this instance, the store had a promotion of doubling coupons. The major difference between this process and the show Extreme Couponing on TLC is that you will not have a basement stockpiled with items that will take years to use. Who needs 46 bottles of sweet relish just taking up space? Instead you'll have what you need, no more no less.

Have at it! Drive the cost of grocery shopping down. Look for the lowest total cost. This may take an hour or two when you first implement this strategy, but it'll get easier and quicker as you get better at it - and the savings will be phenomenal.

Here's a real life example to show how powerful this strategy can be. Between the two of us, we spend $80-100 per week on groceries. That's for two grown men. With that we get seven breakfasts, seven lunches, and five to six dinners. Yes, we take our lunches to work every day. We don't do fast food or quick-casual dining, like our colleagues who are spending $6 to $25 per lunch. We don't do frozen dinners. Our grocery bags are filled with fresh fruits, vegetables and natural, unprocessed meats and fish.

Remember at the beginning of this book when we detailed our individual stories and we talked about our out-of-control spending and how we were regularly spending $400 on groceries on top of dining out? Compared to then, we're now saving $400 a month on groceries and dining out. With that alone, we're saving $5,000 a year. You can start to see how we paid off our credit cards in a little over two years.

We understand that we don't all have the same eating habits. We make our own breakfasts, lunches, and dinners and try not to dine out excessively. We find this approach to be a real money-saver. However, it's the planning that allows us to do this. For those who don't find cooking enjoyable, we suggest trying to prepare one or two meals a week to save from dining out. In a crisis, any savings is helpful.

Our breakfast staples include eggs with salsa that are easily cooked in the microwave (actually quite good). Sometimes we throw a little cheese on top. We sometimes enjoy yogurt and granola with flax seed and fresh berries. Another breakfast that we have is steel cut oatmeal with raisins, cinnamon and slivered almonds that we prepare in advance and reheat in the microwave. Sometimes we throw in some brown sugar. All of these cost less than a dollar a day per person and can be made in two minutes - and they're healthy, unlike the dollar menu at fast food restaurants on the way to work.

Along with each of these breakfasts, we throw in a piece of fruit for good measure. To keep from spending $3 to $4 for a cup of coffee, we brew our own at home or at work. A whole bag of beans and quart of Half & Half come out to about $15 and will last two weeks, where as two weeks of coffee at the local coffee shop will run about $75. That doesn't include all the fancy lattes and designer cappuccinos, either. We splurge from time to time and get a bagel or breakfast sandwich, but by planning a menu, you're ahead of the game, and it's easy to prepare any of these options and save time.

The lunch break in the middle of your work day doesn't have to break your budget. As with breakfasts, have a list of handy meals that you can quickly prepare for your lunches throughout the week. In addition, we regularly use leftovers from dinners as lunches. We understand that many people hate leftovers, but this just requires a shift in thinking. What is a frozen lunch that you get from the freezer aisle? It's a "leftover." It's a meal that was cooked weeks or months before with more salt than one human needs, then flash-frozen and packaged for you to reheat in the microwave.

The alternative to packing your lunch is dining out. True, a nice lunch out is great, but do it every day and you're going to spend $120 a month easily. That's just if you're doing fast food, like McDonald's or Wendy's. $120 a month comes to $1,440 a year. If you invested that same $1,440 each year at 8%, you would have $190,668 after thirty years. As you can see, cooking for yourself can be quite profitable.

There are hundreds of inexpensive and healthy options when taking your lunch to work. How about tuna salad on whole wheat crackers, grilled chicken salads, or a big pot of homemade chili with ground turkey or whole grain spaghetti with sauce, plus soups and anything left over from dinners earlier in the week. Another perk with leftovers is cooking less. Take, for example, the pot of chili. Make it for dinner on Sunday evening; then have enough for a few lunches throughout the week. Bingo, instant lunches!

Dinner, often the last thing you want to make when you get home from a long day at work, doesn't need to be a divine four-course meal every night. For those who've watched Rachel Ray's "30 Minute Meals," you know a good meal can be whipped up quickly, even for a family of four or more. As we've discussed, our dinners can be the bridge to all our lunches for the week. Why not cook once and have enough for three or four meals?

When you grill, throw on six or eight pieces of chicken, rather than just two. When you make spaghetti, use the whole package and have enough for future meals. One of our favorite methods is using the crock pot. Yep, sounds very Betty Crockerish, but it works - and works well. Throw in a package or two of ribs with some barbeque sauce, turn it on before heading to work and - voila! Dinner's ready even before you get home. On top of that, you have a couple of lunches for the week.

Crock-Pots or other slow cookers aren't terribly expensive and are on sale quite often. This is a great household item to purchase with one of the numerous 20% discount coupons that Bed, Bath & Beyond stuffs in your mailbox each month. If these aren't coming to you in the mail, you can sign up online to receive text versions of these 20% discount flyers.

On the next few pages, we have examples of a couple of menus and corresponding grocery lists. We have an example for a family of four and an example for a couple. The only way this is successful is if you stick to your menu. Add a few snacks from time to time, but you don't want to do this often. Why? Because then you end up replacing regular meals with snacks. When this happens your menu is shot and you waste food and money.

Try to avoid prepared or pre-packaged foods. These foods are higher in sugars, salts and fats, and they're overpriced. Take, for example, the pre-packaged envelopes of oatmeal. They may taste good, but a box of 12 costs around $5. If you get a container of quick oats from the bulk section of a grocery store and throw in your own brown sugar, you can get about 40 breakfasts for the same price. This homemade concoction whips up in the microwave in the same amount of time as the pre-packaged stuff.

Take a look at the following menus and grocery lists:

Grocery List for the Menu for the Week

Sunflower		Target	
10 grapefruits	3.34	hair gel	4.00
10 navel oranges	5.00		
8 apples	3.00		
3 lbs red/green grapes	6.00		
4 pints blackberries	6.00		
3 lbs chicken tenders	6.00		
1.25 lbs ground beef	4.00		
ground turkey	3.00		
grape tomatoes	1.00		
3 avocados	1.50	**Vitamin Shoppe**	
cucumber	1.00	COq10	10.00
3 lbs squash	2.40	Vitamin B	15.00
3 veggies	7.00		
OJ	4.00		
yogurt	3.00		
eggs	2.00		
lemon juice	4.00		
pasta	2.00		
sauce	2.00		
teriyaki sauce	3.00		
salsa	3.00		
bran	1.00		
Whole Foods (Whole Paycheck)			
quinoa	3.00		
salmon	20.00		
cod	8.00		
amaranth	3.00		
Total	83.90	Total	29.00
Grand Total	112.90		

Menu for the Week

Sunday –
B – Granola, yogurt, fruit
L – Take-out
D – Grilled chicken skewers, brown rice, veggies

Monday –
B – Eggs w/salsa
L – Lunch date w/ movie
D – Grilled beef burgers, veggies, quinoa

Tuesday –
B – Oatmeal, fruit
L – Grilled chicken skewers, brown rice, veggies
D – Grilled fish, mashed potatoes,
avocado/tomato/cucumber salad

Wednesday –
B – Eggs w/salsa
L – Grilled beef burgers, veggies, quinoa
D – Pasta w/ turkey sauce, veggie

Thursday –
B – Oatmeal, fruit
L – Grilled chicken skewers, brown rice, veggies
D – Grilled fish, mashed potatoes,
avocado/tomato/cucumber salad

Friday –
B – Eggs w/salsa
L – Pasta w/ turkey sauce, veggie
D – Happy Hour @ The Lure Lounge/bite down town

Saturday –
B – Oatmeal, fruit
L – Leftovers
D – Baked cod, amaranth and veggie

You may see items on the menu that are not on the grocery list. These may
have been purchased in bulk in previous weeks.

To help, we've included in the back of this book both a menu and grocery list template.

In summary, here are tips for grocery shopping:

- Create a weekly menu and grocery list.
- Design menus and grocery lists around a combination of coupons and sale items, preferably in tandem.
- Cook as many meals at home as possible; stop lunching or dining out.
- Stay away from processed or prepackaged foods. Consider making foods from scratch; it's actually not that difficult.

How to Have a Date

Remember that scene in *Pretty Woman* where Julia Roberts gets dressed up in that beautiful red gown and Richard Gere gives her a gorgeous diamond necklace - and then surprises her with a flight to New York City for dinner? It was amazing, huh? Julia has never looked better. It was romantic. It was expensive and exciting. But that's not reality – and it's not us. (On the other hand, most of us aren't prostitutes, either.)

For regular people such as ourselves, we can have a nice date, even a great date, without having to be a Wall Street-Baller. There are any number of places you can go and things you can do that won't cost a fortune. It just takes a little creativity and, as always, a little planning.

For starters, look around your own town or city. What does it offer? Do you have a museum? How about parks? Here's an idea: Go on a date to the museum on one of their free days (usually offered once a week, some once a month). Walk around, look, and talk about the art. Talk about what you like and don't like, who's impressive and who's not. Afterwards, grab a NSE bottle of wine and a little fruit or cheese and sit in the park for an enjoyable afternoon.

Is there a decent library in town or a charming book store? You could take your date to the library, grab a book of romantic poems, and go sit at a coffee shop, sipping your coffee and reading to each other. You could also go to the park with that NSE bottle of wine and read.

The reason we mention getting a NSE bottle of wine is because nowadays you can get a quality bottle of wine and not have to spend a great deal of money. One of our staple wines is Black Box Wine. It's a great every-day wine. You can get a box that holds about 4 bottles of wine for $20. That's $5 a bottle. What would it have cost if you had bought that same bottle of wine at a restaurant? It would be triple, if not quadruple the price, just so you can have someone pour it into a glass for you. That's just food for thought, or in this case - wine for thought. An added benefit is that the wine stores better in the box.

Another favorite idea of ours is going to the movies. We know movies are way over priced these days. Here's how to skirt that issue. Go to a matinee or check out one of the plethora of discount movie houses that are around. Who cares if the movie has been out six or eight weeks? There are so many movies out there these days, it's impossible to see them all in the first week or two anyway. So what if the theatre is a bit older? The camera works, and it's a movie you haven't seen. Another super-saver tip: stop at the grocery store to stock up on snacks to take to the movie. At $7 for a tub of popcorn or $4 for a bottle of water, you have to cut this cost somehow. We especially like this because we tend to be healthy eaters and movie theater food is crap.

The only investment recommendation is to buy a copy of *The Entertainment Book* (see www.entertainment.com). It's only a great investment, though, if it gets used. We typically get our money's worth several times over. *The Entertainment Book* has tons of coupons for any number of products or services: movies, fast food, quick-casual restaurants, fine dining, sporting events, travel, ski lift tickets, retail, and all kinds of services. Research it online before purchasing. The book is customized for local areas.

Ours offers coupons to local grocery stores and oil change hubs and any number of things. Oil changes are necessary, right? In the long run, the better a car is taken care of, the less the maintenance costs. The price of *The Entertainment Book* is reduced in February or sometime thereafter. If you can wait, this helps to save even more. You may want to sit tight and get it for half off the regular price.

Let's take a moment to discuss the "coupon." For many there's a stigma with using them. To the uninitiated it can be seen as cheap or stingy. This isn't true. We are in financial services and have worked with many multi-millionaires, and know for a fact that they are *always* looking for a discount. Oprah has even talked about how she is always looking for good deals. If a billionaire is trying to figure out ways to get a discount, then why can't we? The business puts the coupon out for a reason - to get you to buy their product or service. They should be thankful you're doing so. With services like Living Social, Groupon, and Amazon Local, more places are getting into the coupon business. Take advantage of it, but only buy what you need. Nowadays there's almost no reason why you should pay full price for anything.

If you have a craving for a nicer dinner out, go to one of the restaurants that provide a coupon in *The Entertainment Book* or on Groupon. It's easy to have a NSE fancy dinner for two, but only pay the price of one. Don't forget to fairly tip your server based on the original cost of the meal or service, not the discounted price. Getting meals and entertainment at up to 50% off means: one, you're saving more, and two, every once in a while you can splurge and do something a bit nicer and not have to worry about the extra cost (NSE).

On one date, John made a restriction that we couldn't spend more than $20. This turned out to be quite fun. We had a two-for-one coupon at a local ice cream shop. Afterwards, we used two coupons to get into a show at an art house theater. We came in at $22. Even so, it was a great evening that didn't hurt our wallets. We challenge you to do the same.

It pays to look in local magazines and newspapers. If you have a local magazine that lists coming shows and attractions, often they'll have listings of places that are offering good deals or even free events. There's a local restaurant that we love going to on Fridays for happy hour with our friends. They have two-for-one dinner and drinks. It's a top-notch restaurant with great food. We can't beat the price and experience.

On the first Friday of each month, a local art district in Denver has its galleries open for free. DJs spin and many galleries offer free wine and appetizers. For a really fun Friday night, we'll hit happy hour at the two-for-one restaurant and then head over for the art exhibits. It's a great time, especially with good friends. These are some of the ideas we can get from our local paper.

Granted, not everyone lives in a big city, and you may think your own town is boring. In that case, you'll have to use a little creativity. One example is taking advantage of your local movie rental store, streaming service or Red Box. Grab a movie for less than $5, hit the local grocery store for some decent snacks, and have a nice evening watching a movie at home. You can have a quiet and romantic evening for $20 or less. Go Dutch and it's $10 per person.

This isn't all, and our ideas are inspired by staying as close to $20 as possible. Considering inflation and where you live, a $20 cap may not work. The idea is to cut back on the extravagance and still have quality time with the person you love. This is the philosophy behind NSE. The whole point of a date is to spend time together. It's not so much what you do, but who you do it with.

We would love to list more suggestions, but that is a whole other book. Actually it is. Look forward to our upcoming book, *Fifty-Two Weeks of Free*. That being said, here are six date suggestions to inspire you. Each example provides an average cost based on our research.

Date - Dinner and a movie			Date - Museum and wine at a park	
Moe's Southwest Grill			1 Bottle Yellow Tail Merlot from liquor store	$7
2 Burritos, chips-salsa, and 2 Margaritas	$20		Dubliner cheese, apple and olives from grocery store	$12
2 tickets to Movie at Regal Cinema Theatres	$12		Denver Art Museum on first Saturday of the month	$0
2 Chocolate bars from grocery store	$3		(wine glasses and knife from home, picnic blanket)	$0
Total	**$35**		**Total**	**$19**
Date - Sunrise at Red Rocks			**Date - Movie Night In**	
Bottle of Prosecco from liquor store	$10		Domino's Online coupon - three 10" pizzas	$23
OJ, muffins and 2 pieces of fruit from grocery store	$7		Download movie from iTunes	$5
Free entrance to Red Rocks Amphitheatre	free		Six-pack of beer and bottle of wine	$14
Total	**$17**		**Total**	**$42**

Date - Double Date to Denver Nuggets game		Date - Jazz or Concert in the Park	
Family 4-pack of tickets, 4 pizzas and 4 sodas	$59	2 Sub sandwiches - buy one, get one free	$9
4 beers	$24	1 Bottle of Yellow Tail Shiraz	$8
Soft pretzel	$5	1 Bar of Chocolate dark chocolate w/ cherries and Almonds	$6
Parking	$10	Free concert in the Park	$0
Total	**$98**	**Total**	**$23**

In summary, here are tips to having a fun and affordable date:

- Think outside the box – look for things that are free.
- Use coupons – 50% off on meals, movies, and activities will save a lot (like 50%).
- Go for NSE –there are plenty of "not so expensive" options out there, especially when it comes to food and alcohol.
- Staying in vs. going out – Staying in can be just as much fun and you can get to know your date, friends and family just as much - if not more!

How to Vacation

Vacation! Ahhh, we just love that word. A vacation is a break from work and a break from the norm. It's a chance for a great adventure or visit a great destination. Off to the airport, bags packed with an extra one that's empty for the goodies you're going to bring home - plus a wallet or purse in tow. Relax, have fun, shop, eat and drink. What happens though? More often than not you come home feeling like you need a vacation just to recover from your vacation. Funny thing, when typing "vacation" in the previous sentence, David accidentally typed Vegas instead of vacation. Freudian slip?

A few weeks go by and you settle back into (or are thrust back into) normal life. Your mind drifts back to the fun you had and how you wish you could go back for a few more days. Then the mail comes - the Visa bill. You're just a bit scared to open it, but you go ahead. OMG! You spent how much? Two, three, four thousand dollars is not uncommon for vacations these days. A week at a nice hotel can run well over two thousand alone. It was fun, but was it *that* much fun?

Remember how much money you really make? Now think of all the hours you're going to have to work to cover that. For a family of four with a two-person income of $100,000 that goes on a $5,000 vacation, the mother and father will each have to work 100 hours. That's two and a half weeks each for one week of vacation. That's all, of course, if they didn't pay for their vacation with credit and are now carrying a balance. That's enough work to make them want another vacation when this one's paid off.

How do you go on an enjoyable, relaxing vacation without breaking the bank and your back? By now you should know the answer: planning! Seriously, did you expect anything else? Let us describe a recent vacation we had and explain why it felt so good to go - and better when we returned.

Friends of ours announced they were getting married. We were excited for them and looked forward to their wedding. Then they told us they were getting married in Mexico. Fortunately, they told us over a year in advance. They chose an all-inclusive resort, which turned out to be five stars and a great deal. All the friends and family worked with the same travel agent to get packages from Denver, including flight and five days/four nights for just over $1,100 per person. We did the math and figured that if we each saved $100 per month, we could cover it. We needed a deposit of $200 and the balance was due in 12 months. It worked out perfectly. We were motivated to set aside the money from our regular pay and to cut back just a bit on our non-discretionary spending to make it work.

March rolled around and we pulled $2,200 from our bank accounts and BAM! It was paid off before we even went. Additionally, our bonuses were paid in April, so we had a few extra dollars to take with us. Not only was the trip itself a blast, but so was the aftermath knowing that we owed nothing. No expectations of credit card bills, no worries about how long it was going to take to pay off, and the relief in knowing that it was not going to cost us 20-30% more because of finance charges.

In the story above, we illustrate two valuable lessons when it comes to travel. First, have a plan and pay for the trip before going. If you cannot afford to save and go, then don't go. Second, sometimes all-inclusive resorts are great deals. At this resort, everything was included: food, drinks, service, and some activities - it was a very nice resort. It's important to check out what's included, though. Some "all-inclusive" resorts aren't so all-inclusive.

Travel discounts are available everywhere these days. But just because it's listed as a discount doesn't mean it's a good deal. Shop around. For this, the internet has become our best ally. We prefer the sites like www.kayak.com, www.bingtravel.com and www.farecast.com, but there are plenty of others to help you find cheap flights, hotels, and car rentals. Investing time in Google searches will save money. Make sure to only use reputable companies.

There are some keys to saving more. The most important is being flexible. Look for non-peak travel dates. If you can fly back on a Monday or Tuesday, rather than on a Sunday, you can generally save $50 to $100. We look for quality hotels, but not five-star. (Remember NSE.) For example, if you're going to the beach, which hotels are going to be the most expensive? The hotels on the beach will cost the most. If you plan to spend most of your time at the beach, why not pick a hotel that's a block or two away? All you're going to do is sleep there anyway? You'll save $30-60 a night, which you can spend on dinner or the cabana boy for getting you a few more foo-foo drinks.

Another way to plan and lower the cost of a vacation is to book as a group. It may make sense to rent a house and each person/couple take a room, rather than each getting their own hotel room. Often this is better when going with intimate friends or family. There are several great benefits: if you're going with your parents, Mom and Dad may just kick in for most if not all of the cost of the house. Another benefit is having a kitchen. It helps when you can make a breakfast, lunch, or dinner from time to time. Rather than taking a group of six to ten out for dinner at a cost of $200 or more, how about cooking dinner in and going out for dessert afterwards? NSE!

We'd all love to take that amazing trip to Fiji where we get massages every day and dance the night away. Reality is, just like a NSE bottle of wine, a NSE vacation can be just as enjoyable and relaxing. How about some NSE vacation suggestions? Okay, here you go.

Instead of the week-long romantic vacation in Fiji, try a four-nighter at a bed and breakfast within a day's drive of home. If you live in the South or the West, Santa Fe has some great spas and hotels that are not going to cost an arm and a leg. In the East, head to Vermont or New Hampshire for the fall colors and remember that the small, quiet and quaint places can often run hundreds cheaper. This is also where travel-blogs can help. We look for others who have stayed at the same place, so that we can get a feel for whether it is a great deal or if it's just cheap.

Another piece of advice: plan trips to second-tier cities. What are second-tier cities? Second-tier cities are fun, vibrant cities with tons of culture and entertainment, but aren't huge such as New York City, Chicago or LA. These are cities such as Austin, which has a bustling live music scene, Minneapolis and their world-renowned museums, and Portland and its short jaunt to some of the best vineyards and micro-breweries in the world. These destinations have a lot to offer and aren't as expensive as larger cities.

A great tip for NSE vacations is to think locally. Because of high gas prices, 2011 was called the summer of the "Staycation." If time away from work is needed, take a couple of days off and stay home. Sleep in and stay up late. Go out for a nicer dinner or two (maybe to a restaurant with a coupon in *The Entertainment Book*). Rent or go to see a movie, play or musical if you want to do it up. Another idea is to find a local hotel to stay at for a night or two and play "tourist in my town."

The trick is to not get wrapped up in household chores. Stay off your computer and Blackberry and don't think about work. We screen our calls, too. Now you'll know what to tell people when they ask, "What should I do when I come to (insert the name of your city/town)?"

An idea we've taken advantage of is having our employer subsidize part of our vacations. Both of our jobs require some travel, so we piggyback vacations onto these trips. We've taken many extended vacations this way and it saves lots of money. If we're staying at a hotel, they'll often extend the corporate rate for the entire stay. Our employer pays for the one of us who has to travel for work. Because we don't typically travel for work at the same time, we use airline miles earned to fly the other out and compound the savings. If you don't have airline miles, consider flying your partner out on Tuesdays, Wednesdays and Thursdays and on off hours. This can be done for any place you travel to for work. Every place has something to offer, even if the only benefit is being away from home for a few days.

Another tip for NSE vacations is to plan ahead with *The Entertainment Book* (www.entertainment.com). Their website allows you to search for deals in any location by changing the address and zip code. Searches can be done for hotel, restaurant, entertainment, and shopping discounts in any area. This is a great way to save and plan for places to go and things to see and do. Additionally, you can see menus online and print coupons. Saving 10% to 50% per cent on these expenses really cuts costs and still allows you to have a nice time.

If you follow any of these suggestions or have your own, the trick is to plan ahead and save the cash that you'll need. Don't blindly use your credit card, thinking you'll pay it off later.

If the goal is to pay your debt off as quickly as possible, skip the vacation. No matter how many tricks you implement, vacations are still costly. John put a hiatus on his travels while he was paying off his debt, and paid it off much more quickly because of this. Of course, we're realists and know some people can't do that.

In summary, here are tips for having a fun and affordable vacation:

- First and foremost, plan ahead and pay for it up-front, including saving spending money.
- Think outside the box - not all vacations need to be in Florida, California, or NYC; second-tier cities have a lot of fun and exciting things to do.
- Take advantage of friends and family who would like to see you and are willing hosts for a few days (three days max).
- Always look for deals, think of going slightly off-season, or for a shorter trip.
- Remember NSE tricks, such as staying a few blocks away from major attractions, and choosing three and four-star hotels instead of five.
- Staycations can be just as fun and relaxing; do what you would do on a vacation away, but do it at home.

Summary of Living Below Your Means

- First, address the psychology of why you allow yourself to live beyond your means and change that habit.
- Start looking internally, rather than externally.
- Plan!
- Life can still be enjoyable while living within your means if you plan and think creatively.
- Reassess how you shop, entertain, and vacation.

Chapter Seven:

Principle Three: Cash is King

Introduction to the Cash is King Principle

Why is using cash a principle in becoming debt free and living a Money Conscious life? Look at it this way. Cash is like the training wheels when you're first learning to ride a bike. Only after you understand the basics and have learned balance, can you take off the training wheels and begin to ride on your own. Master your spending habits first by paying with only cash, then move to more convenient methods of payment.

Let's take another look at history to see how cash fits into the picture. As we discussed, people used to barter with one another; exchanging one good for another (or many others) to equate to a perceived value. This often proved cumbersome, especially for large purchases, such as a cow, when all they had were apples. One cow seems to be worth a lot of apples. Later people started to use items of scarcity as a measurement of worth, one of the first being salt. Then there was a transition to silver, gold and other precious metals. Finally, cash was created. With this method, the world worked fine for hundreds of years.

Why did this work so well for so long? It's because this system inherently forced people to only buy what they could afford. If they had $5 and needed flour and sugar, they could only buy $5 worth of flour and sugar. If they also wanted eggs, well, they had to wait until later or cut back on the amount of flour and sugar they purchased. People were forced to live within their means.

Eventually credit as we know it was created (and God said, "Let there be credit!") and people began borrowing for all sorts of things. Back then, they were more careful with credit and generally borrowed from someone whom they trusted, such as the general store manager or a local banker. They were compelled to settle debts because they didn't want to lose their standing in the community. As towns became cities, businesses became more impersonal and bankers realized what a great opportunity offering credit was. Moral pressures began to abate, and people started borrowing against tomorrow to pay for something they wanted today.

Our suggestion is to take things back to the beginning, back to the training wheels. Remember when you were kids, your parents didn't just hand you a checkbook or credit card and say, "Spend." Most likely, they gave you an allowance. You received a small amount of cash for doing chores to help you learn the value of a dollar and about spending saving.

Earlier we suggested cutting up all of your credit cards. We hope you did this, but if not, finish reading about this principle and you'll see that this is the best way to go. We're going to present compelling reasons and easy suggestions to wean you off of credit cards and take advantage of cash. Let's see how you can get a 20% automatic savings on all purchases.

Getting an Instant 20% Discount

Think back to the days after the bust of the .com bubble and 9/11 when you watched in horror as your portfolio and wages dropped 10% to 30%. Reflect more recently on the credit crisis when the Dow fell 7,500 and your life savings depreciated even more than after 9/11. Many of us were disgusted and angry. We hated seeing our assets shrivel away like the Wicked Witch after being doused with water.

What most people don't realize is that they do this to themselves every day. You voluntarily give up 10% to 100% of your money without batting an eye. This isn't because a failing, overly exuberant market is crashing around you. It's because you voluntarily give this to retailers, banks and credit card companies. How?

Remember that great pair of shoes you got for 20% off? Remember the awesome fly fishing pole from last summer that you used once? Yep, it is your purchases. But wait, you got those on sale. Yes, you did. You then paid for them with your credit card? Hmmm?!

That great pair of $140 shoes at 20% off ended up costing you $119 after the discount and taxes. Now the loan sits on your revolving credit card to which you make minimum payments each month. At that rate, it'll be five years until you pay off the loan. After five years and a minimum 20% compounding interest, guess how much those shoes will cost you. Are you worried? You should be. They'll cost you a whopping $296.11. Had you paid with cash, you could've purchased two pairs of shoes.

When we buy something, we mentally stop paying for it as soon as we walk out of the store. The reality is we end up paying for it a heck of a lot longer if we used credit. If this is the case, then why do you keep doing it? Why do you willingly anti-invest by paying hundreds to thousands of dollars each year on interest and late fees when it comes to your purchases and not get mad at yourself. But, you want to strangle your financial advisor when they get you a measly 4% annual return in a bear market?

How do you get an instant 20% return on your money? Credit card companies know we are a nation seeking instant gratification. They know that you are more than happy to play the role of Wimpy from *Popeye*, and let you "gladly pay them Tuesday for a hamburger today." They make huge profits from your out-of-control spending and lifestyle. So, if you want to buy that pair of shoes, then buy them with cash and get a discount of 20% and save $177.11. This is why Cash is King.

Using cash is an efficient tool for Living Below Your Means. Because you're using only the cash in your wallet, it's easier to quantify exactly how much you're spending. This makes it harder to spend more than you have. Remember how David kept a credit card for "emergency savings" and John didn't? This allowed John to pay off his cards significantly sooner than David despite John having much more debt when we started. The reason was David would nickel and dime himself and these little purchases add up.

Having the Right Piggy Bank

Now that you're all grown up, you don't really need a piggy bank. . . . or do you? Not only do you need a piggy bank you need the right one. Having moved to a cash-only (this includes checks) lifestyle, it's important to get the most out of the cash you have. How?

There are some features you need when looking for a bank or credit union to hold your non-discretionary and discretionary spending money (emergency savings is kept far, far away). The features you need are listed below:

1. Free online bill-pay
2. Free ATM transactions and ATM fee reimbursement nationwide
3. Free checking with free standard checks (puppies are cute, but not worth the expense)
4. Interest paid on any balance in the checking account

5. No minimum balance fee, if minimum balance not maintained

6. No hidden fees (requires some investigative research on your part)

Why are these features so important? If you're going to set up all of your payments for fixed expenses to go out when your money comes in, then free online bill-pay will help you make sure those checks go out on time and at no cost. We all love free! Be careful, some banks only allow three to five free online bill-pay checks per month before they start charging fees. Make sure to get *unlimited* free bill-pay.

Free ATMs transactions: When you spend only the cash you have and keep that money as cash, you're inevitably going to need to make withdrawals from an ATM or a bank teller. But going to the bank is so twentieth century. Most banks today, however, charge anywhere from $1.50 to $4 per ATM transaction. Double that amount when you're not using your own bank and you could pay $3-$8 to withdraw $20-$60. That is a whopping 7-15%. Why? Right, it doesn't make sense. Therefore, a bank, credit union, or brokerage that doesn't charge their own fees and reimburses fees charged by other banks is imperative. Look for a bank where this is unlimited, not just 2 or 3 times a month, a quarter or as an "introductory offer."

Free checking with checks is important because you'll be doing some of your larger, flexible spending with checks, such as grocery shopping.

Don't add to the cost by having to pay for checks or the service.

Interest-bearing checking accounts: This is a little less common, especially today in the environment of low interest rates, but there are banks that offer this. Do your research and take advantage of it. You might as well get a few percent each month to use this type of checking account. You can earn a few extra dollars a month from this interest. "A penny saved is a penny earned", right? Remember you're in conservation mode, only spending on the important things. Having an extra $20-$40 a year can help. Every inch counts, so tighten up the belt.

No minimum requirement or minimum maintenance fee: This is important because you will likely empty this account each month. Since you're going to pay off all your expenses each month and put as much as you can towards your debt, you'll have a very active account. More often than not your balance will be very low. If you're frightened by the thought of not carrying a balance, you have your emergency savings account for emergencies.

Personally, we like having our emergency savings account, and on top of that, having sufficient funds in our checking account to pay one full month's worth of bills to provide an extra cushion. For those who are able to do so, this may be a strategy to consider once your debt is paid off. You want to establish your emergency savings first, though. In either case, you're going to need to master the art of balancing your checkbook. Not an easy feat for most, but it needs to be done, and we will discuss this more later. You don't want insufficient funds charges (NSF) on your account. One or two of those a month could knock out a whole category of spending.

Now the big question - where is the right piggy bank? There are several national and regional choices. We suggest checking with smaller, local banks and credit unions first. They'll typically have many of the features you need. These institutions have less overhead and subsidize their services with loans. You don't need one now, but you can take advantage of their free services. Credit unions are likely to give you the best interest rate, have lower fees and charge less for loans when one is necessary. As far as institutions on a national level, consider or ING's *Direct High Interest Checking*. Compass Bank's *Build to Order Checking* account has many of these features also, although they do have a minimum balance requirement of $25.

Your time is now. Find the right piggy bank and start saving.

Strategies for Managing Cash

Now that you're only using cash, what is the best way to manage your cash? Cash seems to disappear so quickly. This doesn't have to be the case. You simply need to learn to manage your cash, rather than your cash managing you. Here are a few tips.

We'll discuss in detail later how to build a budget, but now's a good time to lay a foundation. Pull up Excel on your personal computer. In cell A1, add your spreadsheet title. We have "John & David's Budget". You can do "My Budget" or whatever suits you. In cell A3 type "Pay Period 1". In cell D3, type "Pay Period 2". Continue to cell G3 and on until you've divided the number of paychecks you receive per month into corresponding pay periods. In our case, we have two pay periods. An example of this spreadsheet is below.

Starting in row 4 in columns A, D, G, etc., list the names of the billers that are due until you receive a check for the following pay period. In row 4, columns B, E, H, etc., list the amount you pay each month (with a "-" in front to indicate subtraction) for the corresponding biller. For some expenses, such as heat and electric, you'll have to estimate and confirm when you receive that particular bill. When you're finished, all of your billers should be listed on your spreadsheet.

At the bottom of this list, in columns A, D, G, etc., type "TOTAL". In the cell next to the word "TOTAL", in columns B, E, H and so on, use Excel's "AutoSum" feature. AutoSum will sum a range of numbers in a column or a row. In this case, it will be a column. Click in cells in columns B, E, H, etc., next to the word "TOTAL", and then click "AutoSum". Excel selects what it determines to be the most likely range of data. Click "AutoSum" again to accept the range the Excel selects, or select the correct range and then click "AutoSum". Finally, save your spreadsheet using a name you'll remember.

Each payday pull up your dynamic budget in Excel. Log into your online account and pull up your current balance. Your balance should include the amount of your paycheck and additional money left over from the previous pay period. Subtract any outstanding checks; checks you've written but that haven't posted to your account. This is your available cash balance.

Input the available cash balance figure for the appropriate pay period, either cell B3, E3 or H3, etc. Hit enter and your spreadsheet automatically adds and subtracts payments and expenses that you expect during that pay period and it provides you with your final cash balance for the pay period. This is the amount of cash you'll have left over after all your bills are paid. This is your discretionary cash balance. You can use this extra cash for anything, including making an extra payment to your credit card(s), paying any other outstanding loans, saving for retirement, having a little fun - or some combination of these. If you don't have any money left over or have very little, you'll need to make adjustments to your expenses immediately.

	A	B	C	D	E	F
	Format Painter					
	Clipboard	Font		Alignment		Num
	K16	▾	ƒx			
1	**John & David's Dynamic Budget**					
2						
3	Pay Period 1	$3,322.03		Pay Period 2	$3,322.03	
4	Groceries	-$300.00		Groceries	-$300.00	
5	Gas	-$50.00		Gas	-$50.00	
6	Mortgage	-$888.08		Car Loan	-$606.54	
7	HOA	-$400.99		Internet	-$46.99	
8	Car & Home Owner's Insur	-$171.01		Electric	-$34.21	
9	Cell Phone	-$142.19		Gym Membership	-$16.58	
10	Parking & Storage	-$35.00		Student Loans	-$125.42	
11	Minimum Credit Card Payr	-$128.50		Netflix	-$9.68	
12	Brokerage Investment	$0.00		Miscellaneous	-$25.00	
13	Roth IRA Contribution	$0.00		Minimum Credit Card Payr	-$128.50	
14	Miscellaneous	$0.00		Roth IRA Contribution	$0.00	
15				Brokerage Investment	$0.00	
16						
17	Pay Period 1 Discretionary Cash Balance	$1,206.26		Pay Period 2 Discretionary Cash Balance	$1,979.11	
18	Monthly Discretionary Cash Balance	$3,185.37				
19						

The point is to assess your cash flow at the beginning of each pay period. This gives you a clear understanding of what flexibility you have with your cash until the next payday.

Once your budget calculates this for you, pull out your checkbook ledger, notate the direct deposit from your pay in the Deposit/Credit column, and subtract any of your expenses through the current pay period in the Payment/Fee/Withdrawal column. Notating these deductions at the beginning of each pay period will help you not spend money before you need it for bills. Note that looking at your balance online may dupe you into thinking you have more money than you really do. The checkbook ledger budget will show you your true balance.

4: The Four Principles of a Debt Free Life

AU - Automatic Deposit * AP - Automatic Payment * ATM - Cash Withdrawal * DC - Debit Card * FT - Funds Transfer * SC - Service Charge * TD - Tax Deductible

NUMBER OR CODE	DATE	TRANSACTION DESCRIPTION	PAYMENT, FEE, WITHDRAWAL (-)	✓	DEPOSIT, CREDIT (+)	$	BALANCE
		BEGINNING BALANCE					198 04
	01/30	SUNFLOWER MARKET	97 20				97 20
							90 84
	01/31	PAYROLL			3322 03		3322 03
							3412 87
	02/01	MORTGAGE	888 08				888 08
							2524 79
	02/01	HOA DUES	400 99				400 99
							2123 80
	02/01	CAR + HOME INSURANCE	171 01				171 01
							1952 79
	02/01	CELL PHONE	142 19				142 19
							1810 60
	02/01	PARKING & STORAGE	35 00				35 00
							1775 60
	02/01	MIN. CREDIT CARD PAYMENT	128 50				128 50
							1647 10
	02/01	CASH WITHDRAWAL FOR GROCERIES	300 00				300 00
							1347 10
	02/01	CASH WITHDRAWAL FOR GAS	50 00				50 00
							1297 10

We recommend getting all of your bills set up on bill-pay or for automatic deductions. This saves you the hassle of having to make sure each bill is paid on time. No late fees mean more money to pay off your debt. If you like more control over paying bills, set up bill-pay to email you when a bill is due (most companies will allow this, but not all) and to email you when your payment has been sent. This gives you some oversight. An additional benefit is the reduced papers piling up on your desk.

If you're like John, you'll find balancing a checkbook to be one of the hardest things in the world. John's mother is a whiz at this, but this doesn't seem to be a hereditary trait. We'll talk about how to maintain a checkbook in the next section. For now, know that the fewer entries you make in your checkbook, the easier it is to manage. As we described, each paycheck deposit (direct deposit) and fixed expense should be appropriately itemized in your checkbook immediately after receiving your pay. Paying them immediately is wise too.

From earlier exercises, you should have an estimation of your fluctuating expenses. Some of these expenses can't be paid through Bill Pay because they are "point-of-sale" transactions. This means that you pay at the time of purchase. Examples are gas and groceries. Additionally, you'll need spending money. For each of these, we recommend the Envelope System. This is a "highly technical," but simple strategy. Trust us! We have three separate envelopes; one labeled "Groceries," another labeled "Gas," and the last labeled "Spending."

On (or just after) each payday, stop at the free ATM and withdraw all the cash you need to cover these three categories until your next pay check arrives. This means you only have two ATM withdrawals for the entire month if you are paid bi-monthly. This will vary for those on a different pay cycle.

You now have your money for groceries, gas, and for fun. Once it's gone, it's gone. There's no more. This helps you stay within your budget. If you can't find a bank that offers free ATM services, limiting your visits to the ATM will decrease the amount of money you pay in fees. If you don't have access to an ATM, make this withdrawal from your bank teller. In either case, itemize these deductions in your checkbook ledger as soon as these withdrawals are made.

Once you get home, divide the cash among your envelopes according to what you've outlined in your budget. This lets you know what you have available for each category until your next paycheck. Depending on your circumstances, you may have more or less envelopes. You may have one for the babysitter, since teenagers don't typically take credit cards. You may want one for church or other charitable donations, unless you plan on taking a tax deduction for these donations. A check can be your proof for taxes. Our "Spending" envelope holds our entertainment, social, and miscellaneous spending money. Do what works for you.

We know this seems like an archaic and clumsy system. Many "financial experts" will mock it. It works for us and that's why we're sharing it. Complexity and perceived sophistication don't guarantee success. That's what we've found. We do suggest putting your envelopes in a safe place, such as a locked filing cabinet or a fire-proof box.

In the unlikely event that you come to the end of the pay period and have extra cash in any of the envelopes, subtract this balance from what you withdraw for the next pay period. This leaves excess cash in your accounts and away from the temptation to spend it. It's our recommendation to put this extra cash towards your credit cards or other loans, paying them off sooner. If you don't have debt to cover, consider putting the extra cash into a savings account or IRA account. Another option is to make an extra payment to your mortgage lender, requesting that 100% of this payment be put towards principal.

Managing the Dreaded Checkbook

We've mentioned several times in this section that moving away from credit cards and using cash and/or checks is a great tool to help you Live Below Your Means. Using only cash does make this a lot easier, but you may not like carrying large amounts of cash in your wallet. In some cases it doesn't make sense, especially if you have safety concerns.

Checking accounts, on the other hand, have their own considerations. Checking accounts require a higher level of spending awareness. Current online/statement balances don't always reflect an accurate balance. There's a chance you may have already spent some or all of your balance with checks that have not yet posted.

Ugh! Yes, this is where balancing your checkbook comes into play. No need to tear up and cry; it's not that bad. We remember the nightmares of learning this (or trying to learn this) and not succeeding. Result: bounced checks. A bounced check means an insufficient funds fee from your bank and from the merchant. How exactly do you balance a checkbook? It's not that hard.

When ordering checks, order checks that come with a carbon copy. This will give you documentation of when, where, and for how much each check is written. Next, you'll need to get into the habit of regularly adding and subtracting the credits and debits in your checkbook ledger. This will make balancing your checkbook a lot easier. If you add and subtract credits and debits as you go, your checkbook will remain balanced. It's still good to do from time to time, regardless. For one reason, you want to make sure you include earned interest. We balance our checkbook each payday. This helps us plan for the weeks ahead and minimizes the number of ATM transactions we generate. Forget itemizing one transaction and - bam, a FEE!

When balancing a checkbook your itemizing checks that have cleared and tallying those that have not cleared. The example below shows how to do this.

Balancing the Checkbook		
Checks written	Amount of the Check	Check Cleared
#204	$27.10	x
#205	$33.90	x
#206	$35.60	
#207	$109.12	x
#208	$66.43	x
Bank Balance online	$107.55	
Outstanding checks	$35.60	
Available balance in account	$71.95	

In the figure above, John has one outstanding check that has not cleared. That means he needs to subtract the amount of that check from the balance listed in his account online. He subtracts $35.60 (check no. 206) from the $107.55 to come up with

$71.95. $71.95 is the amount of cash he has available to spend.

If you're able to do this at least once per pay period and refrain from spending more cash than you have, you'll keep your spending below your net take home pay. This will prevent you from "earning" bank fees.

One last point; verify the check amount against your checkbook register. This will ensure that there hasn't been a transposition or miss-read error by you or the bank. There have been times when banks have misread checks and deducted more or less than they should have.

In summary, it's important to keep your checkbook balanced if you're going to have a checking account. The key tips are:

- Get carbon-copy checks.
- Get in the habit of documenting every transaction, deposits and deductions.
- Regularly balance, at least once per month (we do ours each payday, twice per month).

Summary of Cash is King

- Not using credit cards for your purchases will give you an instant 20% savings.
- Choosing the right bank and establishing a system of money management that's mostly automatic will help you live Below Your Means.

- Use checks when necessary, always documenting your spending and keeping a current balance.

Chapter Eight:

Principle Four:
Have a Financial Plan

Introduction to Having a Financial Plan Principle

As we grew from being financially unaware to becoming Money Conscious and Living Below Our Means and understanding that Cash is King, we were frequently reminded of the need to have a plan. Have a Financial Plan is the fourth principle in becoming and living debt free.

Financial planning, like the other principles, can seem daunting. But it's only as hard as you make it. When we started living below our means, we had a plan and a simple one – and it worked. When we switched from using credit cards to using cash and checks, we had a plan, and again, simplicity ruled.

The importance of having a plan cannot be overstated. If you don't know where you want to go and what you want to do, then you end up lost. Having a plan is an extension of being Money Conscious. It's a clear and personal map of your financial goals.

What does a financial plan entail? Keeping it simple, we'll look at some basic necessities. Beyond these basics, personalize your plan to meet your individual needs. You're aware of your own capabilities, and personalizing your financial plan will help ensure your success. Here are the basics: understand where you are currently, know where you want to go, and chart the steps to get yourself from here to there. Simple! Let's get started.

Understanding Your Current Situation

It's time to bring together everything you've done so far. First, do a little review of your current situation. In Being Money Conscious, you totaled all of your expenses and calculated exactly how much you're earning. These exercises are going to be the basis of your analysis. Grab those worksheets again and let's do a more thorough review.

Pull out the following worksheets: How Much Money Do I Really Make and Where My Money Goes. You're going to use these to complete the My Current Financial Picture Worksheet. If you couldn't already tell, it's going to show you two bits of information about your current financial situation: one, how much you're spending relative to how much you're earning, and two, how much debt (liability) you have compared to your assets.

Take a look at the following example.

My Current Financial Picture Worksheet

Monthly snapshot

Take home pay: _____$2,489.32_____

Average monthly spending: __$2,753.60_____

Monthly deficit or surplus: _____-$264.28_____
(Subtract spending from take home pay)

Short Term Liabilities

Total credit card debt: __$1,097.15____

Total loan debt: _____$13,500_____

Total: _____$14,597.15_____

Long Term Liabilities

Student loan debt: _____0_____

Mortgage debt: ___$63,385.44___

Total: ___$63,385.44___

Assets

Checking and Savings Accounts: ___$336.44_____

Emergency savings: _____$600.00_____

Value of investments: _____$114.66____

Value of retirement investments: __$52,182.13___

Total:___$53,233.23___

In this example, notice how David was spending $265 a month more than he was bringing home. Where was that difference going? You guessed it, on his credit cards. Initially it's not much money. Although $265 a month over a full year ends up being $3,180, excluding compounding interest. Imagine how quickly that gets out of hand with one or two emergencies. Now it's your turn. Go ahead and complete the worksheet yourself.

My Current Financial Picture Worksheet

Monthly snapshot

Take home pay: _____

Average monthly spending: _____

Monthly deficit or surplus: _____
(Subtract spending from take home pay)

Short-Term Liabilities

Total credit card debt: _____

Total loan debt: _____

Total: _____

Long-Term Liabilities

Student loan debt: _____

Mortgage debt: _____

Total: _____

Assets

Emergency savings: _____

Value of investments: _____

Value of retirement investments: _____

Total: _____

Creating an Action Plan

We hope this exercise wasn't startling, for most it isn't pretty. There are good lessons that can be learned from this exercise. The first is that you gain a perspective of how much you're over-spending each month. This is a perfect starting point for considering ways to reduce your spending. The second is that you get a good look at how much you really owe, especially when it comes to credit card debt and short-term loan debt. If you're going to be debt free, you need to have a plan to eliminate this debt. Lastly, if you look at your combined assets and subtract your short and long term liabilities, you get a picture of your net worth. This number is the *what-would-I-have-if-I-had-to-sell-everything* number. Let's hope that number's positive. You don't include the equity in your home. If you're lucky enough to have equity, than you may be even better off.

Let's go back to your spending deficit. Once you know how much you're regularly overspending, you can determine how much you need to adjust to stop overspending. In our example, David was putting $837.60 per month towards paying off the balance of his credit cards. Keep in mind, he was also overspending by $265 a month and this was adding to his card balances. Imagine how quickly his balances would've shrunk if he didn't add to his cards. In addition, he was paying an average of $24.32 a month to service his debt, which came to almost $300 per year in fees.

Your first step is to have a plan when it comes to your budget. We touched on budgets in Being Money Conscious, but here is where you'll put it into action. Pull out your Where My Money Goes Worksheet. Look at the various categories and compare the percentage of your take home pay that you devote to each category. David's example is shown below.

Where My Money Goes Worksheet

Expense	Dollar Amount	Percentage
Rent/Mortgage	$ 2,217.20	26.84%
Dining out	$ 965.69	11.69%
Car payment	$ 909.51	11.01%
Groceries	$ 888.04	10.75%
ATM withdrawals	$ 544.39	6.59%
Alcohol and Going Out	$ 486.56	5.89%
Travel	$ 467.56	5.66%
Clothing	$ 321.35	3.89%
Miscellaneous	$ 285.00	3.45%
Insurance (auto, home and medical)	$ 237.91	2.88%
Gas	$ 194.13	2.35%
Home (decorating, furniture, other home niceties)	$ 173.48	2.10%
Utilities	$ 190.00	2.30%
Personal Items (hair cuts, dry cleaning, etc.)	$ 145.39	1.76%
Other Auto (oil changes, maintenance and repairs)	$ 106.56	1.29%
Medical	$ 65.26	0.79%

In this example, David spent his money in a number of different categories, some of which were obviously out of balance. Notice how we ranked them based on his percentage of total spending.

What categories in the example are out of balance? We see a couple. How about Groceries and Dining Out? Together these two made up nearly 23% of his take-home pay. That is an awful lot of eating. Either David was a big eater - or he was wasteful. Quality food is good, but spending for gourmet food and shopping at high-end grocers can wreak havoc on your budget. Whole Food's nickname isn't "Whole Paycheck" for nothing.

Let's cut the fat. How do you do that? Take, for example, David's dining out expenses. Looking back at his My Spending Analysis, he had 40 occasions when he ate out over a three-month period. That's once every three days. Many were small purchases, like the $4.52 charge, which appears regularly. A closer look shows these were breakfast and coffee purchases. What if he cut back to one coffee shop visit per week and stuck to the breakfasts he bought at the grocery store for the rest of the week? Looking at some of his grocery purchases, there are plenty of trips totaling $10 to $12 dollars. These are impulse purchases, satisfying a yearning for popcorn or ice cream while watching TV.

He cut both categories by 20%. This alone cut about $125 of overspending per month. That's nearly half of the $265 we're shooting for in cutting his expenses just to break even. How could we make this work? Since we moved to a "Cash is King" philosophy, our plan takes $321.90 from dining and cuts that by 20%, leaving $257.52. We'll drop that to $250. Each pay period, then, we withdraw whatever difference we need in order to match that: $125 because we're paid twice a month. If we were paid weekly, we would withdraw $57 a week. We put it into our cash envelope, and only use it when we go out for dinner. We'll do the same for groceries; our budget cut takes us to $236.87 a month. Our next step is to budget for that amount.

We're only 45% of the way there. What else is out of balance? The next item is the most common and deadliest to your debt free life, and that's ATM withdrawals. This is something we call our "Ca$h Hole". Why? Because we withdraw the cash and it disappears into a black hole. Gone! No idea where we spent it. It gets sucked out of your wallet. In addition, you're paying fees for this? Because of this, we propose leaving the ATM card at home. Make ATM withdrawals once per pay period. Fewer transactions mean less fees and less of a probability that you'll spend your money on something stupid. David cut this category by 90%, taking only one $20 transaction as a lapse in judgment or an emergency.

There we go. He has an additional $160. Add this to his $125 from savings groceries and dining out, and there's $285 in savings. Following those two simple steps, David is on his way to living below his means and making great strides to pay down his credit card balances.

It's not going to be this easy for everyone. Some will need to take drastic measures to cut spending. It may not be 20% or 30% out of a few categories. It may be that you need to cut *most* categories across the board. This may not be possible in categories of rent/mortgage or auto loans. You may have to live with a poor decision to buy a house you can't afford or a car you shouldn't be driving. Maybe you need to downsize or right-size, meaning selling the house or car you have for something more practical. Owning a home isn't appropriate for everyone. Some are better off renting. Some are better off driving a five to ten year old car or taking the bus.

What if your situation requires that you take *drastic* measures? Let's look at the Alcohol/Going Out category in David's example. David was spending over $150 a month. We broke out this category specifically for the under-35 crowd because this is the time when most go out regularly searching for "The One" - and we're not talking about Barack Obama. You may need another way of find "The One." What good are you going to be to someone if you saddle them with debt at marriage?

We're trying to make that point that you may need to make significant changes to your lifestyle. Because it's hard to be honest about your spending and make cuts where necessary, we're providing a list of items to consider cutting:

1. Reduce or eliminate cable TV – save $20-100 per month
2. Cut back your cell phone plan – save $5-50 per month
3. Change the daycare center your children go to – save $80-400 per month
4. Eliminate after school activities for your children - $25-250 per month
5. Quit smoking – save $20-100 per month

6. Stop having your hair colored at a salon - $100-200 per month
7. Cut or stop subscriptions to magazines - $5-10 per month
8. Cut back on cocktails and going out - $50-200 per month
9. Live with the clothing you have - $100 -200 per month
10. Get a medium cup of drip coffee instead of a fancy latte - $20-40 per month
11. Play golf at a public course rather than a private one - $50-100 per month

Let's take a look at two possible plans for David, one where only a slight reduction in spending is needed and one where drastic cuts are needed.

	Current Spending	New Budget		Current Spending	New Budget
Rent/ Mortgage	$739.3	$740	Rent/ Mortgage	$739.3	$740
Utilities	$63.43	$65	Utilities	$63.43	$65
Entertainment	$20.84	$50	Entertainment	$20.84	$20
Dining Out	$321.9	$255	Dining Out	$321.9	$40
Groceries	$296.09	$235	Groceries	$296.09	$230
Clothing	$107.25	$105	Clothing	$107.25	$0
Gas	$64.83	$65	Gas	$64.83	$65
Personal Items	$48.33	$50	Personal Items	$48.33	$50
Car Payment	$303.27	$300	Car Payment	$303.27	$300
Travel	$155.88	$100	Travel	$155.88	$0
Medical	$21.67	$25	Medical	$21.67	$25
Misc.	$94.88	$95	Misc.	$94.88	$20
ATM Withdrawals	$181.33	$20	ATM Withdrawals	$181.33	$20

Alcohol/G oing Out	$162.16	$100	Alcohol/ Going Out	$162.16	$20
Home	$57.71	$60	Home	$57.71	$0
Insurance	$79.3	$80	Insurance	$79.3	$80
Auto			Auto		
Other	$35.44	$35	Other	$35.44	$35
Totals	$2,753.61	$2,380	Totals	$2,753.61	$1,710
Total Savings	$373.61		Total Savings	$1,043.61	

Notice the two budgets and the savings with each. In both cases, we cut back well over $350. In the first, we cut the major categories that we discussed earlier and cut travel: dining out, groceries, ATM withdrawals, alcohol/going out. Notice, too, that we increased our entertainment category from $20 to $50. If we're cutting back on going out, we need to spend our time doing something. Adding a bit to entertainment will allow us to keep busy with NSE entertainment and not break the budget. This scaling back allows us to have a decent standard of living, but also puts about $4,500 annually towards David's credit cards and other debt.

In our example, where drastic changes are necessary, we cut almost all of David's non-essential spending. We cut in the same categories, such as dining out, groceries, ATM withdrawals, alcohol/going out, but to a much greater degree than in the previous example. We cut travel, home, and clothing completely - something most won't like. When it comes to choosing between keeping our condo and traveling to Paris, we think most would say, "Keep the condo!" If not, go back to the beginning of this book and start reading it again. You missed something.

It's your turn. Fill out the My Spending Reduction worksheet below.

My Spending Reduction Worksheet

	Current Spending	New Budget		Current Spending	New Budget
Rent/ Mortgage			Rent/ Mortgage		
Utilities			Utilities		
Entertainment			Entertainment		
Dining Out			Dining Out		
Groceries			Groceries		
Clothing			Clothing		
Gas			Gas		
Personal Items			Personal Items		
Car Payment			Car Payment		
Travel			Travel		
Medical			Medical		
Misc.			Misc.		
ATM Withdrawals			ATM Withdrawals		
Alcohol/Going Out			Alcohol/Going Out		
Home			Home		
Insurance			Insurance		
Auto Other			Auto Other		
Totals			Totals		
Total Savings			**Total Savings**		

It's time to create your dynamic budget. The first few months after doing this, you'll need to do a regular check-up and make adjustments to make it work. Remember that your objective is two-fold. One goal is to create a budget and the second is to build something you can live with. Your dynamic budget should become a way of life. When we did ours, it didn't take more than two or three months before our spending habits changed, and it became a way of life.

My Dynamic Budget Worksheet

	Amt.		Amt.
Pay Period 1		**Pay Period 2**	
Groceries		Groceries	
Gas		Gas	
Mortgage/Rent		Car Payment	
Cell Phone		Internet	
Insurance		Gym Membership	
Utilities Sewer		Utilities Electric	
Utilities Gas		Student Loans	
Health & Beauty		Utilities Water	
Children's Activities		Dry Cleaning	
Clothing		Charity/Church Donations	
Miscellaneous		Miscellaneous	
Minimum Credit Card Payment		Minimum Credit Card Payment	
Brokerage Investment		Roth IRA Contribution	
Roth IRA Contribution		Brokerage Investment	
Pay Period 1 Discretionary Cash Balance		**Pay Period 2 Discretionary Cash Balance**	
Monthly Discretionary Cash Balance			

Debt Payment Plan

Now that you've created a plan to cut your spending, it's time to put your extra money to work in cutting your debt. That's the main reason you're cutting back your spending in the first place isn't it?

The first step in creating a debt payment plan is to contact your credit card companies and negotiate a lower annual percentage yield (APY). You'll need to be clever and aggressive (but not rude) here. If you're in sales, this will be easy. If not, remember that like He-Man, we have the power. Credit card companies make most of their money charging you interest. If they think you'll take your business elsewhere, they'll be more than willing to negotiate.

We suggest searching the Internet and calling credit card companies to research the rates and terms being offered for consolidating debt, i.e., charges to consolidate, length of the introductory rate, annual fees, etc. Once you're armed with the information you need, contact your current credit card companies, tell them that you appreciate their services, but their fees are too high and you're going elsewhere for a lower rate.

Silence is golden. The person on the other end of the phone is human, too, and silence on your part can be deafening on theirs. Another tip is to know what rate you want and ask for better. This gives you room to negotiate. Finally, remember that you always have the power to walk away from the negotiating table and to take your business elsewhere.

Once you've negotiated a lower rate or consolidated to a card with a lower rate, get a clear picture of your debt and what your "amazing" friends at these credit card companies think is a reasonable term for paying your debt off. Next, you're going to measure their suggested payment plan against your own plan. You'll quickly see the benefit in following your own plan.

Having your own plan and sticking to it will save you hundreds, if not thousands, of dollars. A debt payment plan allows you to create goals towards becoming debt free, charting a clear and definable path to success. It, also, provides benchmarks for incremental rewards.

How do you build a debt payment plan? Look to your credit card friends for advice on how to build this. First, you need your most recent statement for each of your credit cards. From these you need the statement balance and the suggested monthly payment, and then somewhere in the fine print you should be able to find the "purchase APR." This is the amount of interest you're charged on an annual basis for new purchases. Most likely this will be anywhere from about 14% to 30%. Yuck, remember the "Getting an Instant 20%" section? It's time to start getting that back!

With these numbers, create a column for each credit card, a column for its current balance, and one for the minimum monthly payment. Next, total the Current Balance and the Minimum Payment columns, to get your total owed and the total you are being advised to pay each month. This figure is pretty miniscule compared to what you owe, right? Divide the total of the Current Balance column by the total of the Minimum Payment column. This gives you a rough estimate on how long it will take to pay off each card. This does not include interest, which you'll pay until each card is $0. For now, this rough calculation will work. Take a look at the example below.

My Debt Payment Plan Worksheet				
Credit Card	Purchase APR	Current Balance	Minimum Payment	Months to Pay Off
Chase United	13.99%	$1801.98	$42	42.9
Banana Republic	22.99%	$193.67	$10	19.4
Totals		$1995.65	$52	38.4

In our example, David had a $52 required minimum monthly payment. Paying the minimum with no additional purchases or finance charges, it would've taken over three years to pay off both credit cards. Three years! If he added the finance charges, it would've taken close to five years. That's too long.

If you go back to the budget we created for David, you'll remember that by modestly reducing dining out, grocery shopping, and eliminating the non-budgeted ATM withdrawals, we came up with an additional $373.61 each month in extra money. This is money to apply to the debt each month.

Your first goal is to see if you can pay off any cards immediately or within three months. We suggest doing this because it'll give you instant gratification for making immediate progress. When you finally cross a credit card off your list, it's a great feeling. You'll cut up the card, throw the pieces away and ask for the account to be closed. Done! Your second goal is to get rid of the cards with the highest finance charges. The less finance charges you pay, the more you can put towards your debt. That's more money for you and less revenue for your banks.

This is pretty easy. In our example, David can pay off his Banana Republic card in one month because of his reduced spending and then switch all of his payments to his Chase card. His commitment is to do this on a regular basis. As discussed in the Being Money Conscious section, this needs to be considered a fixed expense paid regularly through Bill Pay. In the above example, David will now have a monthly commitment to pay a total of $373.61 towards his cards. We suggest making payments based on when you're paid: weekly, bi-monthly, or monthly. David is paid on the 15th and the last day of the month. As a result, he'll divide his payment as follows:

| Banana Republic | | | | United Visa | | | |
Month	Balance	Payment	New Balance	Month	Balance	Payment	New Balance
15-Nov	$193.67	$165.8	$27.87	15-Nov	$1801.98	$21	$1780.98
30-Nov	$27.87	$27.87	$0.00	30-Nov	$1780.98	$158.94	$1622.04
15-Dec				15-Dec	$1622.04	$186.8	$1435.24
31-Dec				31-Dec	$1435.24	$186.8	$1248.44
15-Jan				15-Jan	$1248.44	$186.8	$1061.64
31-Jan				31-Jan	$1061.64	$186.8	$874.84
15-Feb				15-Feb	$874.84	$186.8	$688.04
28-Feb				28-Feb	$688.04	$186.8	$501.24
15-Mar				15-Mar	$501.24	$186.8	$314.44
31-Mar				31-Mar	$314.44	$186.8	$127.64
				15-Apr	$127.64	$127.64	$0.00

Notice that we have the debt from the Banana card paid off in one month, and the debt from the Visa card paid off in five and a half months. That's a lot better than doing it over three years, as suggested by David's credit card companies. Keep in mind that he will be paying some finance charges. For this reason, we expect to extend the payment of the Visa card an additional payment or half a month.

Based on a simple amortization schedule, we figure that David will pay about $60 in finance charges over this six-month period, whereas paying at a constant $42 per month would end up taking 58 months to pay off - with a total of $643.02 in interest charges. That's right! David would pay over $600 in finance charges (based on the monthly-compounding, not the daily-compounding that the majority of cards use today). This is the reason a debt payment plan makes sense. Please take the time to create a debt payment plan for yourself with the Debt Payment Plan worksheet below.

My Debt Payment Plan Worksheet

Card Name				Card Name			
Month	Balance	Payment	New Balance	Month	Balance	Payment	New Balance

In the beginning, it'll seem daunting to have so much debt to pay off. If you make it a habit to pay off as much as you can each month, you'll see progress in no time. Making progress is a lot easier if you *stop* using your credit cards and *only* use cash going forward. Otherwise, you run the risk of building up as much (or more) each month as you pay down, as David did.

The last step in creating a debt payment plan is to stop letting credit card companies badger you with their too-good-to-be-true offers. By calling 1-888-567-8688, you can request that the four major credit bureaus stop selling your contact information to credit card solicitors.

Below is the contact information to the Direct Marketing Association. By contacting them, you can request to be taken off the distribution list of all telemarketing and junk mail. Not only will this save you from aggravation and temptation, but it'll reduce paper waste.

Mail Preference Service
Direct Marketing Association
P.O. Box 9008
Farmingdale, NY 11735
1-800-407-1088
www.optoutprescreen.com

To opt out of other telephone solicitation lists, send your complete name, address, and phone number to:

Telephone Preference Service
Direct Marketing Association
P.O. Box 9014
Farmingdale NY 11735

Finding Other Sources of Income

Here's an interesting topic. Everyone wants more money, but it's not necessarily easy to earn more money. We'll start off with our personal favorite; start your own small business.

This is beneficial for a number of reasons. Not only can you make more money, but you get the practice of starting and running a small business. Additionally, if you itemize your activities correctly, you can write off some of your expenses against your taxes. You know that personal computer that you have? With your own business, you can write off some of its value against your taxes. Do you have an office that you don't really use? Well, use it to run your small business and you can write that room off against your taxes. Now you're working and making money for yourself rather than someone else, and the government's going to give you a break to do it. Excellent! An additional benefit that we must share is that the more time you spend working, the less time you have to spend money. It helps both sides of the balance sheet.

What if you don't know what to do? There are thousands of options. We started an online T-shirt business. It was easy, fun, and educational. We didn't have to invest a lot of time or money. However, it provided us with a lot of experience, satisfaction, and a little extra money.

Go into business doing something you love. If you knit blankets like John's mother, knit blankets and sell them on www.Etsy.com. John's mother gets requests all of the time for her handmade blankets (a lot from her son to use as wedding gifts). If she charged for these, she would do well.

If you sew, sew for others. If you like gardening and manicuring yards, do yard work for others. Clean houses. Babysit. If you're good with typing, type a college student's paper. If you fix your own computer, fix someone else's. Take as little business or as much business as you like. That's one of the many benefits with being your own boss. Don't over-think it. Don't assume that what you love doing can't make you money. There is money to be made. Check out www.taskrabbit.com or www.craigslist.com as a place to advertise your services or products.

If starting your own business isn't your cup of tea, put in more time at your current job. Most employers are in dire straits looking for more qualified employees. Use their problem to your advantage. Do overtime and earn time-and-a-half (or even more with some companies). Even just a couple of hours a week can add a nice bit to your paycheck. Plus, your boss may see that you're eager and hard working and this could have long-term benefits for your career, which brings more money. Plus did you know that working just one hour of overtime a week is like getting a 3.75% raise?

While we're on the topic of your current employer, another trick to freeing up cash is to increase your deductions on your W-4. This should be possible by contacting your Human Resources department. Most people put 0 or 1 down for their deduction and enjoy receiving a large refund each year after they file their income taxes. This is fun, but by doing this you're only loaning money to the government for free since they don't pay interest on this money. Increase your deductions so you get more money with each paycheck. Your new deduction should allow you to either get very little in return after you file your taxes or make you owe very little. Talk with an accountant to determine the best deduction for you.

A final option is finding a part-time job in addition to your current one. Make the most of it. If you love coffee and spend $40 a week at Starbucks, get a job at Starbucks and get yourself a discount - or even free coffee. If you love concerts or movies, work at an arena or movie theater. If you work in a grocery store, you'll get a discount off your regular groceries. We don't recommend that people who are addicted to shopping work in stores where they actually enjoy shopping because this is getting too close to the fire. You could get burned by spending all the money you make on merchandise from that store.

Finally, if your spouse stays at home for any reason, it may be time for them to pick up a paying job. If they're staying home to raise your kids, maybe they can babysit one or two more children. Maybe they can grab a part-time job or start one of the small businesses mentioned previously. It's the whole family's debt, so the whole family should participate in paying it down.

Another caveat on top of the shop-a-holics working in retails stores is any get-rich-quick scheme. They should be avoided at all costs. Stay away from any sort of gambling, including cards, race tracks, slot machines, and so forth. Finally, there are millions of ads online or even posted around town offering a great life of working from home for only a few hours a week and promising an "executive salary" with little work. Remember to trust your instincts. If it sounds too good to be true, it is. You don't want to put yourself into a worse situation than you already are. Most of these offers require money upfront to get started, which isn't worthwhile in most cases.

There are honest companies that will let you work from home, set your own schedule and let you work a few hours a week or as many as you like. Great resources for finding these jobs are:

- www.momslikeme.com
- www.workingsolutions.com
- www.alpineaccess.com

Keep in mind that you're not going to make millions from these work-from-home businesses, but they can be a great tool to supplement income. Alpine Access, a company listed above, pays about $9 per hour; a relatively easy and cheap way to add $50 to $100 a month to your income - and do it from home.

Whatever your situation, there's something that you can do to bring in extra money. It may take some thinking outside the box, altering your current routine, or taking on a little more than you're used to, but it'll be worth it. Who knows?

You may find yourself a new career or you may find out that you're pretty good at running a small business - and would like to make it a big business.

Focus on the Goal

We wrote this book with the goal of helping others get on track financially. We know that living the principles of Being Money Conscious, Living Below Your Means, and understanding that Cash is King, and having a Financial Plan is the easiest way to get there. As you create your financial plan, focus on the the goal.

Our debt payment plan was an example of this. We set a realistic timeframe to pay off all of our debt, worked towards it, and achieved our goal. What a great feeling it is when you accomplish a goal! There are two things we must add. The first is that you need milestone rewards built into your plan, and the second is that you need to prepare for your lifestyle transformation while you're paying off your debt.

Having milestone rewards and a lifestyle plan are going to be the fuel to getting you to your goal. First we're going to discuss how to reward yourself when you achieve milestones - without sinking yourself further into debt and by avoiding the proverbial one-step-forward, two-steps-back effect. After this, we'll discuss creating a "new" lifestyle plan.

Milestone Rewards

Working to pay off your debt will be a fun, exciting and liberating process. Trust us, it does get better! The most excitement comes when you reach a major milestone. What are these? They depend on the individual. Here are a few suggestions though: paying off all of your credit cards that have a balance of $500 or less, paying off *all* of your credit card debt, reaching the half-way point in paying off all your short term debt, and becoming completely debt free.

As you can see, these milestones will depend greatly on personal circumstances, but are similar objectives for each of us. Reaching these benchmarks should, alone, provide inspiration for you, but you didn't get here without sacrificing. Because of this, we suggest rewarding yourself when you achieve defined milestones.

You're trying to pay down your debt. There are two important qualities about milestone rewards to avoid regressing. First, the reward has to be paid for with cash, and second, the reward should not be so expensive that you get off course.

What kind of rewards do we suggest? Here are a few ideas:

- Getting a massage at a local massage school where the cost is a lot less than a professional massage.

- Taking yourself out to dinner and a movie (remember to use coupons for both and the NSE).
- Buying yourself something special that you've had your eye on for a while - maybe an article of clothing, something small for your home or office (this shouldn't blow your budget, but be a visual reminder of reaching your goal).
- Taking a get-a-way that's close to home (drive somewhere for the day, taking the day off and get away from it all).
- Cooking a special dinner for friends and family that have been supportive of you. (They will relish your success and be that much more supportive of your reaching your goal completely.)

What about the final milestone? Going all the way? We know you'll get there. It's going to happen. What will you do when you reach the "finish line?"

We celebrated big when we reached the finish line. We timed it with our trip to Mexico for the friend's wedding that we mentioned earlier. Because we knew where our finish line was, we were able to plan eleven months in advance and save up all the cash we needed for the big trip. It was exciting for us to go to a friend's wedding in Mexico. But the most exhilarating part was being rewarded for finally becoming debt free!

We suggest that you do the same when it comes to rewarding yourself. Make *major* plans using cash. Don't buy something that will go away – instead, make it a lasting memory. Take friends and family out for a special dinner, buy a special piece of art (something that will hopefully increase in value and also be a reminder of what you accomplished), or take a vacation. You've achieved something significant that justifies a reward whenever you build a life for yourself that's free from debt. That's a major accomplishment.

Keep in mind that you'll need to save and reward youself with all expenses covered with cash. This is how having a plan helps. We suggest planning and saving well in advance. Start setting money aside into a special savings account; add it to your emergency savings account or an investment account. The point is to prepare and save for it so that you can make it big. It will help motivate you.

Your Lifestyle Plan

To truly make the change from happenstance and frivolous spending to knowing where your money goes and guiding you to make the best purchases, you must have a lifestyle plan. A lifestyle plan helps you to continue to live the life you enjoy, but at the same time focus on doing it not so expensively (NSE). It helps you change your habits and then helps you benefit from your new habits. You start to think and spend differently. Right now many of you may be saying, "But I don't want to change my lifestyle." Uh, yeah, you do - you *do* want to make a change. This may, in fact, be the best change you'll ever make.

There are many aspects to consider when building a lifestyle plan. You need to consider entertainment, shopping, home life, milestone rewards, holidays, vacations, and so much more. A valuable lesson we learned early on about a lifestyle change was how valuable the plan is. No plan, nothing to do. Nothing to do means boredom. When we were bored, the first thing we found ourselves doing was spending money on things that didn't help us achieve our financial goals - things we didn't need and couldn't afford. Whether on food, entertainment, or mindless shopping at the mall, we would spend money one way or another to satiate boredom.

When you don't know how you're going to spend, you're more likely to spend more than your budget allows. For example, on a typical Friday night after work, if we don't plan to cook dinner at home and get a movie and stay in with friends, we'll likely go to happy hour, spend $40-$60 on a few cocktails, then head out for dinner and spend $40-$50 each. By nine o'clock, we don't know how the night is going to end and we've already spent $80-$110 apiece.

Planned dinners at home with friends, a movie and a six-pack, or a couple of bottles of wine would cost us about $50 total - and we can split that among four people. For that matter, we can foot the bill from time to time and still win. Just remember your friends are not charity cases, you don't need to become their soup kitchen. Look for a healthy balance when splitting costs.

Know what your options are and have a plan. Keep a few coupons in your wallet or car for places where you dine and shop. This will help at the spur-of-the-moment when you go out with friends or family. You want to control the number of times you have these moments. This means being prepared with a plan and sticking to it. Okay, what does a plan look like?

Here's a look at our calendar for one month. We planned specific activities that will help keep our costs down, but still remain involved with our friends while we enjoy entertainment and relaxation time.

February 2011

Monday	Tuesday	Wednesday	Thursday	Friday	Saturday	Sunday
	1 Rent a movie ($4 – Social Network)	2	3	4 First Friday Art Walk (Free)	5 Denver Art Museum (Free)	6 Superbowl Party @ Friend's House ($15 Food & Beer)
7	8	9 Professional Networking Event (Free) Drinks at Event ($20)	10	11	12 Dinner Party for 8 @ Our Place ($100)	13 Grammy Party @ Neighbors ($15 Food)
14 HOA Annual Meeting	15	16 Joy Wine Tasting (Free)	17	18 Matt Morris @ Bluebird Theatre ($40) After show drinks ($40)	19 Jenn's Baby Shower ($20)	20 Colorado Mammoth Lacrosse Game (4 ticket Party Pack w/ hotdogs and beer - $25)
21 President's Day	22 Movie: Blue Valentine ($30)	23	24 Rooms Board 2011 Furniture Collection show (Free)	25	26	27 Oscar Party @ Friends ($20 wine)
28						

As we mentioned earlier, after a few weeks or months, something seems to happen with your spending habits. You go through a transformation. Like working out and changing your eating habits, your body and mind become accustomed to new patterns. You become internally motivated to work out and eat right. Spending is exactly the same. When spending, you start to ask yourself, "How will this impact my budget; do I need this?" Because you now only shop for what you need.

You gain a level of confidence. You live consciously. You walk into a store and buy only what you went there to buy. You can go to the mall and only buy what you intend. You develop an internal guide that reminds you that this is good for you, for your family, and your future. After a year or two, you'll start to see the world, material things, and the emotion of shopping differently. You'll recognize what's good for you. The most rewarding part is it will become second nature and enjoyable. And guess what? This is when you start to become rich! Not just with material things, but with confidence and security.

Emergency Savings

Hmm, the word "emergency" is a scary word. It brings to mind car accidents, broken bones, a burning house, or natural disasters. Attach the word "savings" to "emergency" and what happens? The context changes. "Emergency savings" is the security blanket for your life.

The two words together mean that if you get into a car accident, you have a financial cushion of protection. If you break a bone, ouch! But you won't break the bank with medical bills. If you lost your house in a fire or natural disaster you'll be emotionally devastated, but not financially devastated. If you lost your job today, you will have a personal safety net. You can make it for a few months - or even longer - with your emergency savings. You're prepared financially. You won't be like the hundreds if not thousands of Federal employees furloughed in the 2013 government shutdown, who went on eBay or Craigslist to sell personal belongings just to make it through to the next paycheck.

Sound like a pipe dream? It doesn't have to be. Emergency savings is just that: your savings for an emergency. Sadly, most of us are living paycheck to paycheck. One hiccup and you're in debt up to your ears. An extended set back and you're close to bankruptcy. Why cause this stress in your life? Why trade this freedom and security for a new flat screen TV or a Coach handbag? Would you exchange the bag or TV for a few months of security? We hope so. If you want that security now, plan and save for it now!

This should be your next financial goal after paying off your debt. We feel strongly about this because without it, you're only one paycheck away from being in debt again. How do you get this savings? Make a plan, of course. That's exactly what you'll do right now. Let's think for a moment about potential emergencies, so that you can be prepared for them financially.

For most of us, especially in this economy, one of our first concerns is losing our job. How much do you bring home? How much would you need if you quit, were laid off or fired? Many states are "at will" where an employer can fire you without cause.

Your job isn't guaranteed, and you need to be prepared for what may come.

How much is the deductible on your insurance, whether medical, life or other? You have insurance, right? What if your deductible is $250, $500 or even $1,000? Do you have enough saved to cover it? How much do you need to help with all these concerns? Pull out your most recent budget again.

How many of us are certain to find a new job within two weeks? Whether in good times or bad, this can be difficult. One of our highly skilled fathers was out of work for over a year trying to find a new job after he was laid off. Luckily, he had emergency savings. (Dad was right, again!) Because of unforeseen circumstances, we suggest saving anywhere from three to six months worth of living expenses.

Why the range? If you're relatively healthy and have worked for the same company for a while, you shouldn't need more than three months worth of savings. If you have health issues, are new to a job or working in a volatile industry, it helps to have closer to six months worth of savings.

Take all of your monthly expenses from the dynamic budget spreadsheet you created and total them. Add in your contribution to your retirement and savings accounts and multiply this total by three or six. We recommend continuing to save for your future during hard times, if possible. If you can't because of your situation, this is an added cushion. In some situations, you won't pay taxes.

Create a strategy to accumulate this savings over time. When you build your Debt Payment Plan, you should consider building in small contributions on a regular basis to your emergency savings account of up to $300-$500 to act as a small emergency savings reserve. Afterwards, put all extra cash towards your debt to pay it off quickly. After all of your debt is paid off, finish building your emergency reserves.

Put this cash in a secure, yet liquid investment. Most people put their emergency savings in an interest bearing account or money market. You want to be able to access it easily, in case of sudden or unexpected surprises.

Don't get a debit card or check-writing on this account. You don't want it so easily accessible that when you're at Best Buy and find a new flat screen that you like; you decide it's an "emergency" because the sale ends today. You no longer buy on impulse.

We have our emergency savings at a credit union. We started with small $25-50 per paycheck investments and increased this over time. Forego a movie or a few cocktails a month to make room for this. The best part is that after just a few months, we started feeling secure. It's a great feeling.

Believe us, you'll appreciate having this money once it's saved and set aside. We should, also, mention how fluid your cash flow is when you're saving money, rather than when you're paying down debt. It's psychological, but it makes saving enjoyable.

Paying It Forward - What to Do with Your Excess Cash

Go ahead, laugh! When are you ever going to have excess cash? You will, especially as you get closer to paying off your debt. If you have a plan and stick with it, you'll make progress, slowly at first - and then quickly. It'll happen. The more progress you make and the more your lifestyle becomes one of Living below Your Means, the more money you'll have available. When that opportunity comes, what should you do with your excess cash?

Some may think this discussion should've been part of the Emergency Savings section, but we think it stands on its own. We believe this because an Emergency Savings account may be a difficult concept to handle.

Paying It Forward is just that - taking a bill that's due each month and paying it ahead by one month. Start with something small like a phone or utility bill and always be ahead one month in payments. It's freeing to have bills, such as your mortgage or rent, arrive in your mailbox and see that the "payment due" is ZERO. It reduces a lot of stress even though you still need to make monthly payments.

We love it, especially with our mortgage payment. When we were finally ahead on our mortgage (it took us many months of small payments to get there), it was exhilarating. What a relief to know that if either of us lost our job, we're one month ahead on our mortgage and still have emergency savings.

Another benefit of this is the power it provides in your life. If you're one month ahead on all your bills, you can be a bit more of a risk-taker when it comes to things like searching for a new job, investing, and devoting extra time to other money-generating endeavors.

For example, when things are tight, how likely are you to spend time scouting for a better job? What about taking a few weeks off to start a small business or work on a book? Not going to happen? Pay It Forward and realize all the freedom, safety, and opportunity that come with this tool.

Paying it Forward is not for everyone, but we have other valuable suggestions to consider for your extra cash. One instance when you'll have extra cash is when you receive a pay raise or bonus. For many, this time comes once a year. What do we typically do when we get a pay raise? We immediately start spending it, but now we're Money Conscious.

At this point, you should be solidly grounded with your budget so that when the extra 2% to 5% comes, you can immediately direct it into something that will make you more money. Why increase your spending when you really don't need to spend more? It's time to get wealthy.

Hopefully, through this whole process, it was never necessary to stop investing in your company retirement account. For most, their company sponsored retirement plan is a 401k, Simple or SEP IRA, or maybe a 403b plan (if you are in government services or teaching). The most important thing to remember about an employer-sponsored plan is that your employer likely contributes to your retirement account if you do. This is FREE money! Most employers match your contribution up to a specific percentage or dollar amount. For example, they may match dollar for dollar up to 3 or 4% of your salary or contribute $2,500 if you do.

When contributing to an employer-sponsored plan, find out what you need to do to get the full match and start doing it immediately. If you can contribute the max of $17,500 (as of 2013 for a 401k) a year as set by the government and get your employer-match, you could potentially invest more than $20,000 a year. This isn't possible for everyone. But when you do see a pay raise, increase your contributions by a few percentage points rather than taking the entire amount of "new money" home - and possibly blowing it.

For fun, the table below shows how your money will grow over 3 years with various contribution amounts and interest rates to an employer-sponsored plan. This doesn't include an employer-match. The second table shows a rate of 8%, which is about the market norm, invested over 3, 5, 10, and 20 years. At the end of 2010 the market rate of return for the Dow Jones Industrial Average was 11.2% over the past 25 years. The sooner you start, the more time you have to grow your money.

Compounding Interest Chart - Invested over 3 years				
Amount Invested Monthly	3%	5%	8%	10%
$50	$1,910	$1,986	$2,104	$2,185
$100	$3,820	$3,972	$4,207	$4,369
$250	$9,551	$9,930	$10,518	$10,923
$500	$19,102	$19,861	$21,037	$21,846

Compounding Interest Chart - Invested at 8%				
Amount Invested Monthly	3 Yrs	5 Yrs	10 Yrs	20 Yrs
$50	$2,104	$3,802	$9,387	$29,654
$100	$4,207	$7,603	$18,775	$59,308
$250	$10,518	$19,008	$46,936	$148,269
$500	$21,037	$38,016	$93,873	$296,538

If you're not lucky enough to have an employer-sponsored plan, then save for your retirement on your own. Open an IRA or Roth IRA account. Talk to a stockbroker or an accountant to determine which is appropriate for you. These accounts allow you to contribute a maximum of $5,500 (at time of print) annually.

Choose a brokerage firm or a mutual fund company to do your investing. If possible, invest online to keep the costs down. The fees for a financial advisor can be high, especially if your balance is low. For starters, consider buying an S&P 500 index fund if you have more than 10 years to retirement or a balanced mutual fund if you have less than 10 years. This is general advice. If you need more customized attention, consider working with a broker or do more extensive research.

A few brokerage firms or mutual fund companies include the following: TD Ameritrade, Scottrade, Vanguard, or American Century. Most of these firms have little or no minimum requirements when automatically investing regularly, and they don't charge ongoing fees. Plus, you can manage your money online.

The topic of investing is a book in itself. We'll get you started in the next section, but look out for our book on the topic of investing in the future.

Retirement

Ahhh, retirement! Some of us picture a crotchety old man or woman complaining about their pills and wondering if they're going to have enough money to pay the electric bill. Others see grandma and grandpa scooting around in a golf cart, clad in neon leisure suits on a Boca Raton par 3. Others see retirement as jetting around the world visiting landmarks, hiking trails in the Amazon, volunteering for the Peace Corps, spending time with grandchildren, and doing all the things they always wanted to do.

Most of us will retire someday. We'll either do so voluntarily or someone or something will force us. We all have our own definition of retirement and what we want it to look like. Most of us want to enjoy the second half of our lives. We say "second half," but for most it's only a few years. It should be a second half, but too many have to work into their sixties or seventies nowadays.

How can you be sure to have the retirement you want? Be clear about the retirement you want and make a financial plan to get there. You have to be financially prepared. Retire too early and you may need to return to work. Fail to be prepared for an emergency or unexpected healthcare costs and you may end up being taken care of in a manner you had not intended.

In the previous section, we recommended participating in a company-sponsored retirement account. We touched on contributing what you can to get your employer-match, but why not max out your retirement completely, contributing as much as you can afford?

Think back to the table of compounding interest in the last chapter. There are two major benefits with company-sponsored retirement plans. First is that contributions to these types of accounts decrease taxable income, and second, the growth in them is tax-deferred.

What does this mean? For every dollar invested in a retirement plan, your tax responsibility decreases by a dollar. Wealthy people take advantage of tax loopholes - and this is a tax loophole for all working Americans. Take advantage of it. Tax deferment means money grows year over year, but you don't pay taxes on the growth until you start to withdraw the money. Generally, this is done in retirement. The less you pay in taxes, the more you have for yourself, your family, and your retirement.

For most, the more we work, the more we make; the more we make, the more we're taxed. In retirement, income typically goes down. As it goes down, income taxes decrease. Of course, this fall into a lower tax bracket doesn't happen for everyone. Consult a tax professional to find out the path you are on.

The most common company-sponsored retirement account is a 401k, although in the public sector you will find a 403b or 457. They are similar in objectives. As of the time of this writing, $17,500 can be contributed into a 401k per year. This is a fair chunk of change. Most plans offer a variety of mutual funds for investing. Diversify your portfolio among large-cap and small-cap mutual funds, international funds, and cash and/or fixed income funds, depending on your level of risk tolerance and time horizon. This allocation should include a mix of index and actively managed funds.

When choosing the actively managed funds, focus on the performance of that fund and the annual operating expense (AOE). AOE is the fee the mutual fund manager charges for managing the mutual fund. You don't want to pay more than you should. Speak with a financial advisor or contact a brokerage firm for guidance. We list several suggestions at the end of this section.

If, after maxing out your contributions to a company-sponsored plan, you have more money to invest, consider investing in either a traditional or Roth IRA. The rule of thumb is that if you're single, or married and filing jointly, and earn above $100,000 annually, consider a traditional IRA. If you earn less, consider a Roth IRA. For traditional IRAs, you can sometimes deduct the contributions from your earned income, thus lowering your taxes. You'll pay taxes when you take your money out. With Roth IRAs you don't deduct the contributions from your income, but you do get to take the funds out tax free after turning 59 ½. Speak with a tax advisor to determine which is appropriate for you.

These accounts typically allow you to trade stocks. If you want to try your hand at trading, trade in a retirement account. The tax impact will be minimal. Be aware that you can lose it all. Stay away from tax-advantageous mutual funds and bonds in retirement accounts, as there are no benefits with these investments in an account that is already tax sheltered. You cannot get a tax break on a tax break.

If you still have money left to invest after maxing out a company sponsored plan and a retirement account, invest this money into a brokerage account. This account is taxable and allows you to invest in most anything. We recommend reserving this account for long term investments. These are investments held for a year or more. Long term holdings have a lower tax rate, plus the less you sell, the less you pay in taxes altogether. Contrary to our strategy with retirement accounts, it may benefit you to consider tax-advantageous investments in this account.

Notice a theme here? The Warren Buffets of the world decrease their taxable income. This is almost as important as how long you invest. Notice how we haven't mentioned anything about picking the right stock or finding a hot stock? Hot stocks are few and far between, and chasing them is no way to invest. Most investors made their millions with well researched, long-term investing. Successful investing is about how long you invest, the regularity with which you invest, and the diversification of your investments – not stock picking. Make researching your investment choices a habit. If you don't have the time, knowledge, experience, or desire to research and choose your own investments, find a professional to help.

For most, the closer we get to retirement, the more conservative our investments should become. As you get older, put more of your portfolio into fixed-income assets: cash, bonds, or certificates of deposit (CDs), which help protect from major swings in the market. Never go completely out of the stock market. Staying in the market generally helps you beat inflation.

Once you start withdrawing from your accounts, it's best to work with financial and tax professionals to maximize your investments and decrease your taxable investment income. You'll eventually move your company-sponsored retirement accounts to a Rollover IRA. This sounds complex, but it's not. It is, however, best left to a professional so that it's done right and without incurring unnecessary expenses.

When it comes to investing for retirement or other financial needs, let others make the big decisions. This doesn't necessarily mean hiring an advisor, but you should let someone who knows a little bit more help you. The easiest way to do this is by investing in mutual funds. Mutual fund managers make beaucoup bucks to manage a pool of millions (and sometimes billions) of dollars.

Most mutual funds permit small initial investments with additional, regular investments over time. This incremental investing of small amounts over time is called "dollar cost averaging." Invest $50 or $100 a month into an account and each month that money is used to buy more shares in the mutual fund of your choice. Remember the compounding interest table? This is the same idea. Even investing $50 a month into a moderate risk mutual fund returning 6% annually will grow to $636 after one year, $2,025 after three years, $3,585 after 5 years, and about $8,400 after 10. Keep putting it away and watch it grow.

Because we don't have the space in this book to discuss all of the ways to plan for retirement, below are some valuable resources.

Retirement Resources

Retirement calculator

- http://moneychimp.com/calculator/retirem ent_calculator.htm

Retirement advice

- http://money.cnn.com/retirement/guide/index.html - multitude of articles and answers

- http://www.americanfunds.com/retirement/index.htm - tools and explanations

Brokerage and mutual fund services

- www.etrade.com – 800.387.2331
- www.vanguard.com – 877.662.7447
- www.americancentury.com – 800.345.2021

Budgeting & Expense Tracking

- www.mint.com

Investing In Your Future

It's obvious we both work in financial services because of how much we focus on saving and planning for the future through retirement and individual investing. Like the cobbler's kids with no shoes, we were failing financially while helping others reach their financial goals. We changed that. We're saving for our future and putting money aside for rainy days, special purchases, and fun times.

Investing may sound boring, but it's not. It's an adrenalin rush. The excitement we felt from paying off our credit cards and watching our debt disappear is nothing compared to the feeling of watching our wealth grow. Seeing investments increase as rapidly as credit card balances once did is thrilling and it's motivating to invest more.

How will it feel to have all of your debt paid off and an extra $20,000 in your bank account? It's a surreal thought, right? Imagine the sense of pride you'll have. You'll develop an amazing level of self-confidence. It's like walking into your class reunion knowing that you're the one that people will look at and say, "Damn, when did she get so hot?"

It feels good to be secure for retirement - or that you're safe if anything unfortunate occurs. As your net worth grows, your debt's eliminated and, hopefully, your income increases. You'll notice a difference in how you feel and how banks, lenders, and others treat you. When all your financial categories are healthy, you can get lower interest rates for homes and car loans, which saves a lot of money in the long run. To us, this is better than qualifying to become a member of some posh country club, though that wouldn't suck.

Here are some resources to help you get started:

Read:

- Burton G. Malkiel's *A Random Walk Down Wall Street*

Online Resources

- www.CNBC.com
- www.cnn.money.com
- www.americanfunds.com

- www.marketwatch.com
- www.fidelity.com

FICO II

Earlier we discussed FICO scores. Because of the impact this score can have on your financial life - not only while you're paying off your debt, but after - let's finish that discussion.

FICO scores range from 300 to 850 and the higher your score the better. Lenders have more confidence that you'll pay back the loan, which translates into lower interest rates for you. This makes larger purchases, such as cars and homes, cheaper. FICO scores are based on five categories: payment history, amount of debt, length of credit history, new credit, and types of credit used. To date, the median FICO score in the U.S. is 723.

FICO scores above 700 are considered "good to excellent." A FICO score between 680 and 699 is typically considered "good." A FICO score between 620 and 679 is considered "creditworthy," but not excellent. Those below 620 are considered a "credit risk" and may find it hard to get a decent interest rate for a loan or get a loan at all. If your score is below 620, consider if now is the best time to take out a loan. It may be better to wait, improve your score, and then get a loan. This strategy, though frustrating, may save you lots of money.

Of the many things that can affect your credit score, the most detrimental is falling behind on paying bills. If you miss making a credit card payment, not only does your variable interest rate with that credit card company rise, but your credit score falls - making it more difficult to get a better rate from another lender. One missed payment and lenders view you as a credit risk. In fact, many lenders and credit card companies have systems to increase your interest rate with your first missed payment, and it doesn't even need to be a payment missed with them. Miss it at another company and (Bam!) interest rates increase. Thus, the reason we suggest automating your payments. If you get into a situation where you think you may miss or be late, contact the card company immediately to see if arrangements can be made to help you.

Another concern is having more available credit than necessary, i.e., having too many credit cards or cards with high limits. This puts you in the situation to easily accumulate too much debt. As a matter of fact, the average American has around nine credit cards. Why does anyone need nine credit cards? It may be wise to consider, especially as you pay them off, closing some accounts or decreasing the available credit. This can help increase your FICO score. Two good rules of thumb are to not have more than 10% of your annual income in available credit and always keep the balance below 50% of what's available. This means closing those accounts strategically.

Lastly, another detriment is having your credit score reviewed or pulled frequently over a short period of time. This generally happens when you're shopping for a loan or applying for a credit card. When lenders see a lot of activity on your credit report, they know you're shopping. This makes them worry. When they worry, your FICO score can drop. Therefore, try to limit the number of times you have your report pulled. If you're in the market for a car, get a loan from a bank before you start shopping. Rather than going from dealer to dealer and having each check your score, prepare in advance and your score is only checked once.

FICO scores are dynamic. Even if you have horrible credit now, you can easily and quickly improve it. How? The best way is to pay your bills on time, especially loans such as mortgages and credit card debts. Another way to improve your score is to pay off your credit cards. When you drop your credit balances below 50% of the maximum balance, your score improves. Be careful to not completely erase your credit history. You need a credit history for any mortgage or car lender to review; otherwise you'll need a co-signer. That would be a drag! Over time, close zero-balance accounts, but retain the credit card account with the longest history.

Another method for increasing credit scores is to pay off your card each month. If you pay off your balance before the statement's due-date each month, lenders notice. Since you've paid all your cards off and are living below your means, you won't need to borrow as much.

In the earlier FICO discussion, we suggested contacting each of the credit rating agencies (Equifax, TransUnion and Experian or www.annualcreditreport.com) to obtain your credit report. Let's take a look at them now and get into the habit if reviewing your credit reports annually.

When you get your credit reports from each of these agencies, you'll want to go over them with a fine-toothed comb. Make sure all the information is 100% accurate. Check your current phone number and address, as well as your address history, and all the credit cards you've owned. If you see credit cards on your report that you've never carried, file a correction with the agency. If you have negative marks on your report that are accurate, plead your case as to why these should be removed. If you have inaccurate marks on your report, file a correction with the agency and explain how you corrected the situation. They should remove these marks - in turn, improving your score. The websites for each of the credit rating agencies or this one: www.annualcreditreport.com, provide instructions on how to file a correction.

Repeat this exercise annually, like filing your taxes or changing the batteries in your smoke alarms. It's not hard and keeps you on top of your game. The FACT Act amendments to the Fair Credit Reporting Act entitle you to one free report from each of the three credit reporting agencies every twelve months.

You can request a free copy if you're unemployed and plan on applying for a job within sixty days, if you receive public welfare, or if you have reason to believe you're a victim of credit card fraud. If you've been denied credit, insurance, employment, a government license or benefit, or the opening of an account, you can get a free copy. Of course, each of the three agencies will *sell* you as many reports as you want if you don't meet any of the above criteria. The cost is around $10.

Philanthropy

Our motivation for paying off our debt was two-fold. Our first goal was that we wanted to build wealth. Our second was to help make the world a better place for those less fortunate. Philanthropy, or the active effort to promote the welfare of others through giving, has an amazing affect on people. When you spend your time and money on others, you get a feeling unlike any other. Think of the efforts to help the victims of hurricane Katrina, the tsunami in Indonesia, and the earthquake in Haiti. We came together as a world community. It was a time when our brotherhood and our values shined.

If you give regularly, you can have that feeing indefinitely. We like to support local charities. In Denver, Project Angel Heart, of which there are chapters around the country, focuses on getting meals to terminally ill people. The first time we worked at the food kitchen we saw the commitment and value that this organization provides, while not wasting money. Ninety-two percent of all donations go to those in need. Now, we take pride in participating in events that support this cause and donate regularly to support it.

Philanthropy, like many other ways of spending your money, is something for which you need to plan. Many employers allow an automatic deduction from your paychecks to send money to a specific (or even general) charitable donation account, which in turn, funds charities. You can also contact a charity, organization, or church and ask them the best way to contribute. As with investing, donating is easier when it's deducted from your paycheck automatically. Remember too, that many employers will match charitable donations dollar for dollar up to a certain amount each year. This is a great way to maximize your contributions.

Reach out to others and find a way to support your local community and beyond. You'll feel better for giving back.

National and international organizations that take automatic donations

- www.redcross.org – The Red Cross
- www.liveunited.org – The United Way
- www.kiva.org – KIVA – Helping impoverished people around the world create sustainable businesses for themselves

- www.clintonglobalinitiative.org – Helping people around the world face poverty, disease, and violence

This is How We Do It - Living the Principles

We've outlined four principles to live a debt free life. Principles do no good unless you live by them. If you live them, you'll reap the rewards they bring. In the world of science, a "principle" is an ingredient, such as a chemical, that imparts a characteristic or quality. What characteristics or qualities will come from adding these four principles as ingredients to your life?

The first chapter talked about how your life will change when you become debt free. It talked about the emotions of joy, happiness, freedom, and pride that will flourish within you. You imagined the capabilities you'll have - spending meaningful time with your family, not getting caught up in the desperate desire to have more, but instead enjoying your life by using your time and money for a greater good.

Another theme woven through these principles is the idea of taking control of your desires and letting go of other's expectations. You're in control of your life. You're at the helm.

All this is true. All this can happen. It will happen!

We know getting started is hard, so start slowly by adding a bit of a principle here and a bit of a principle there. You'll start noticing improvements immediately. They'll be small improvements, yes, but you'll see them. Just like when making cookies or bread, you can't throw all the ingredients in the bowl at once and begin stirring. You need to add them slowly and methodically; so, too, with these principles. We suggest a strategic plan to blend all of the ingredients together, add them a bit at a time, and keep adding. Add and review. Add some more. Follow the recipe, and it will turn out great.

12-Week Recipe

We learned these principles over a long period of time. It took us a while to figure out what ingredients needed to be added and when. We don't want you to have to go through the same trial and error process we did. We've come up with a plan to spare you.

Below, we've broken down the four principles into a 12-week program of adding and measuring, and adding again. Each week introduces you to more and more of the many suggestions we've outlined. We've eliminated the guesswork of implementing these principles into your life.

This is a commitment, and that's exactly how we start the first week. Remember that you are responsible for where you are today, and you are now deciding where you're going to be tomorrow. Debt free!

Week 1

- Sign the commitment contract with a witness (10 minutes)
- Cut up all credit cards except for one (5 minutes)
- Grab all of your bank and credit card statements, pay stubs, W-2, mortgage statements, brokerage and retirement account statements (30 minutes)
- Complete the My Spending Analysis worksheet (2-4 hours)
- Do not spend anything on discretionary spending for the whole week
- Re-read Principle 1 – Be Money Conscious (2 hours)
- Review pay stubs to determine how much you really make (30 minutes)

Week 2

- Complete the My Current Financial Picture worksheet from the book (30 minutes)
- Complete the My Spending Reduction worksheet (1 hour)
- Eliminate excess spending/services (2 hours)
- Sign up for Sunday paper (15 minutes)
- Contact credit rating agencies to request credit scores (15 minutes)
- Re-read Principle II – Live Below Your Means (2 hours)

Week 3

- Complete the My Dynamic Budget worksheet (1 hour)
- Complete the My Debt Payment Plan worksheet from the book (1 hour)
- Re-read Principle III – Cash Is King (1 hour)
- Cut up final credit card (1 minute)
- Set up envelope system (30 minutes)
- Purchase *The Entertainment Book* or similar(15 minutes)

Week 4

- Create monthly activity calendar – focusing on "in-the-back-pocket" dates and free activities (1 hour)
- Plan for a major expense, if needed (15 minutes)
- Re-read Principle IV – Have a Financial Plan (1-2 hours)
- Create a menu and grocery list based on the sales flyers of nearby grocery stores (2-3 hours) *Now start doing this every week from now on!*

Week 5

- Find a credit union, bank or brokerage to house your non-discretionary and discretionary accounts and start an emergency savings account (if possible start with $500 or begin a regular direct deposit of $25 or more per paycheck)

- Establish direct-deposit
- Establish bill-pay and get a checkbook
- Create and review spending for previous month – My Spending Analysis Worksheet
- Re-read Additional Keys to Money Consciousness in Principle I; re-read Creating an Action Plan and Emergency Savings in Principle IV

Week 6

- Find additional ways to reduce excess spending
- Update My Spending Reduction worksheet
- Re-read The Psychology of Living below Our Means

Week 7

- Re-read Budgeting is a Way Of Life in Principle I and Create a Debt Payment Schedule in Principle IV
- Re-assess and adjust My Dynamic Budget worksheet
- Re-assess and adjust My Debt Payment Plan worksheet

Week 8

- Create next month's calendar – focusing on *FREE*
- Re-read My Lifestyle Plan in Principle IV

- Build a list of NSE (Not So Expensive) activities and small purchases we can replace our old spending habits with (wine, entertainment, and food)

Week 9

- Re-read Knowing Where My Money Goes in Principle I and Cash Is King, Principle III
- Create and review spending for previous month – My Spending Analysis Worksheet

Week 10

- Re-read How to Have a Life, including How to Grocery Shop, How to Have a Date, and How to Vacation in Principle II
- Find additional ways to reduce excess spending
- Update My Spending Reduction worksheet

Week 11

- Reread What to Do with Our Excess Cash and Investing in Our Future in Principle IV
- Re-assess and adjust My Dynamic Budget worksheet
- Re-assess and adjust My Debt Payment Plan worksheet

Week 12

- Reread FICO II in Principle IV
- Analyze and correct FICO statements
- Create next month's calendar – focusing on *FREE*

Get started on your new debt free life today!

Menu for the Week of:

Sunday

Breakfast –
Lunch –
Dinner –

Monday

Breakfast –
Lunch –
Dinner –

Tuesday

Breakfast –
Lunch –
Dinner –

Wednesday

Breakfast –
Lunch –
Dinner –

Thursday

Breakfast –
Lunch –
Dinner –

Friday

Breakfast –
Lunch –
Dinner –

Saturday

Breakfast –
Lunch –
Dinner –

Grocery List (in Excel)

	A	B	C	D	E	F	G	H
1	Store Name			Store Name			Store Name	
2	Item(s)	Price Total		Item(s)	Price Total		Item(s)	Price Total
3								
4								
5								
6								
7								
8								
9								
10								
11								
12								
13								
14								
15								
16								
17								
18								
19								
20								
21								
22								
23								
24								
25								
26								
27								
28								
29								
30	Store Total			Store Total			Store Total	
31	TOTAL							

References

1. http://money.howstuffworks.com/personal-finance/real-estate/mortgage14.htm
2. Creditcard.com survey, January 2010
3. Associated Press March 2010
4. http://www.fico.org/WhatIsACreditScore.aspx
5. http://articles.latimes.com/2005/aug/15/health/he-capsule15
6. http://www.boston.com/news/local/articles/2005/12/29/for_lottery_winners___dollars_and_a_little_change_for_many_fortune_is_a_very_mixed_bag/
7. http://www.usatoday.com/news/health/2002-12-08-happy-main_x.htm